CONTENTS

PARADISE ON EARTH
THE GARDENS OF WESTERN EUROPE

Gabrielle van Zuylen

DISCOVERIES

HARRY N. ABRAMS, INC., PUBLISHERS

In the beginning, God created a garden called Eden. Eden is traditionally located in Mesopotamia, probably in the northern part of the region since an apple tree was able to grow there without irrigation. Before the Fall, Eden was a fertile, fragrant oasis of delight, magically calm except for the sweet sounds of water and laughter. Since the dawn of civilization, humankind has ceaselessly endeavored to recreate this mythical paradise.

CHAPTER I

THE GARDENS OF ANTIQUITY AND THE LEGACY OF ISLAM

Trees have been associated with both sacred power and sensual pleasure since the beginning of recorded history. A love of nature permeates the frescoed Garden Room from Empress Livia's villa near Rome (1st century BC, opposite); while the imprint of an Assyrian seal (right) illustrates the spiritual significance of trees as the focal point of a religious ceremony.

Mesopotamia: The Fertile Crescent

The concept of the garden as a place of beauty rather than a strictly utilitarian plot of land first came to Europe from the East. Early in the 3rd millennium BC, Gilgamesh, the mythical king of Sumer in ancient Babylonia, sang the praises of a city graced by gardens and orchards. A thousand years later all the kings in Mesopotamia boasted royal gardens that could serve as regal settings for their banquets and ceremonies; shade trees and flowering plants grew in the inner courtyards of their palaces. Early records describe temple gardens where fruits and vegetables were grown to provide offerings for the gods and, in all likelihood, sustenance for those who served them.

Ornamental pools, date palms, and a wide variety of exotic plants were garden elements at least as early as the 18th century BC: witness this wall painting of a royal orchard from the palace of Zimri-lim on the Euphrates (above). Royal account books indicate sizable expenditures for feeding a large staff of palace gardeners. A stone relief carving (left) from the palace of Sargon II in Assyria shows the king and a courtier hunting in an enclosed "pleasure garden," which would have been stocked with wild bulls, lions, ostriches, and apes. These *paradeisos*, which were part park, part hunting preserve, were planted with flowering shrubs and native and imported trees, including cedar, olive, oak, cypress, ebony, ash, juniper, tamarisk, pine, terebinth, pomegranate, pear, apple, and fig.

The Gardens of Nimrud

By the 1st millennium BC, there is evidence of large public parks in Assyria. Ashurnasirpal II (ruled 883–859 BC) diverted mountain water through a rock-cut channel to irrigate his garden in Nimrud, planted with grapevines and a wide variety of trees, including apple, pear, quince, almond, cedar, and cypress. Some were native species, but many had been brought back from military campaigns as seeds or saplings. The Assyrian king Sargon II (ruled 721–705 BC) created royal hunting preserves outside his city and stocked them with lions and other game. When his son and successor, Sennacherib, moved the capital to Nineveh along the Tigris, he laid out gardens and parks and even attempted to recreate the marshlands of southern Babylonia there. Herons came to nest in his simulated environment, indicating that his efforts proved successful.

A Wonder of the Ancient World: The Hanging Gardens of Babylon

The most famous gardens of ancient times were those at Babylon. According to the historian Josephus, Nebuchadnezzar II (ruled 605–562 BC) had them built for his homesick wife, who longed for the wooded mountains and hills of her native Persia. This rising succession of verdant terraces was considered one of the seven wonders of the world and was praised in literature for centuries.

Tall trees sprouted from the fabled Hanging Gardens of Babylon (below), in its day the epitome of the nonutilitarian paradise garden. As a display of power and wealth, the Hanging Gardens were the precursors of Hadrian's Villa at Tivoli, the Alhambra at Granada, and the gardens of Versailles. The ancient Greeks and Romans were deeply impressed by the gardens of Babylon; the mausoleum of Augustus in Rome, a circular structure with cypresses planted at its summit, was no doubt inspired by the Hanging Gardens.

Egyptian Gardens

The world's oldest pictures of gardens come from Egypt, home to a very ancient garden-making tradition. However, Egyptian gardens were never planted solely for pleasure; they produced wine, fruit, vegetables, and papyrus. As had been the case in Mesopotamia, the emergence of urban civilization in Egypt prompted the development of market gardens to supply food for people living in cities or barren desert regions. The transformation of farm gardens into retreats that could be at once self-supporting and pleasurable stimulated the building of country estates. The layout of these estate gardens was simple: a high enclosing wall to shield against

desert sand, the yearly flooding of the Nile, and intruders; a rectangular central pool; and an orderly arrangement of tall, shade-giving trees. This basic plan remained virtually unchanged for centuries.

Botanical Spoils

The practice of importing foreign plants, trees, and seeds in order to enrich local botanical stocks reaches back to ancient times. Egypt provides us with the earliest evidence of a campaign specifically aimed at collecting exotic plants. In 1495 BC Queen Hatshepsut (ruled 1503–1482 BC) dispatched Prince Nehasi to the land of Punt (modern Somalia) to bring back "incense trees." The expedition sailed from her palace at Deir-el-Bahari and proceeded up the Nile, across the Red Sea, and

Tuthmosis III (ruled 1504–1450 BC) collected many exotic plants during his military campaigns, especially in Syria. No fewer than 256 different species are pictured in the reliefs carved into the walls of the Botanical Garden, a room in the Temple of Amun at Karnak (left).

A glowing description of a garden—including a vineyard, a large pool, and fine trees—is inscribed on the walls of a tomb belonging to an Egyptian governor of the Northern Delta district in the 26th century BC. Judging by a Theban tomb painting from the time of Tuthmosis III (left), this traditional garden layout survived intact for over a thousand years. Reeds and papyrus were cultivated along the edges of a central pool and routinely harvested to make baskets and writing material. Small models of gardens (below) were placed in tombs and accompanied the dead into the afterlife.

on to the Gulf of Aden. Mission accomplished: Thirty-one young frankincense trees were carefully brought back in wicker baskets and planted in the garden of the Temple of Amun at Thebes. The Assyrian invasion in the 7th century BC, the period of Persian rule (6th century BC), and the conquest of Egypt in 332 BC by Alexander the Great fostered the dissemination of exotic species.

Greece: The Original Arcadia

With its rocky, mountainous terrain and hot, dry climate, Greece today appears ill-suited to systematic garden-making, but it was once—before excessive sheep-grazing depleted the land—green and fertile in parts and planned gardens are known to have existed there as early as the 4th century BC. The Greeks originated the concept of the "sacred grove," an unspoiled natural woodland blessed and cherished by the gods, eternally sacrosanct and pristine without human intervention. This lyrical, hallowed garden was diametrically opposed to the philosophy that nature is supposed to be profitably worked and managed. The ancient Greeks did cultivate green vegetables, and wheat was grown for making bread; but flowers grew for the gods. The natural gardens that abound in Greek mythology—from the garden of the Hesperides, where the daughters of Atlas guarded Hera's golden apples, to King Midas's fabulous rose garden—exemplified the ideal *locus amoenus* (or pleasant place), distin-guished from the rest of the natural landscape by its unearthly atmo-sphere, its *genius loci* (or pervading spirit). It was in such magical places, often dedicated to particular gods or heroes, that nature revealed its sacred presence.

Genius Loci: The Spirit of the Place

The Greeks were second to none at taking full advantage of existing topography. The siting of temples, theaters, and agoras was calculated to provide not only natural protection but awe-inspiring views. Trees, with their mystical or divine associations, were customarily included in such settings. The earliest evidence of a formal garden was discovered on the slopes adjoining the Temple of Hephaestus in the Agora in Athens:

As part of an annual summer ritual, Greek women climbed to the roofs of their homes and set out pots of short-lived plants— "Gardens of Adonis"—in memory of the beautiful spirit of vegetation who died so young, during a hunt. The anemone is said to have sprung from the drops of his blood as he died. This seasonal rite can be glimpsed in the fragment of a vase painting at the left.

Two rows of shrubs or small trees, complemented by small narrow beds of flowering plants, were aligned with the building's columns. In addition, grapevines may have grown against the stone precinct wall. The planting pattern of this 5th-century BC Doric temple was undoubtedly typical of classical sanctuaries, which are thought to have been shaded by rows of cypress, plane, or laurel trees.

This Minoan wall painting discovered on the island of Santorini evokes ceremonies associated with nature and the natural landscape. The highly stylized scarlet lilies in the wall painting and the flower held up so delicately in the carving

below attest to the fundamental importance of flowers in both the religion and art of the Aegean. Their colors, shapes, and scents took on symbolic meaning and came to be identified with particular gods, dates, places, or events.

Philosophers and Gardens

As shelter from the sun was a practical necessity in Greece, shade trees were planted near gymnasia, markets, and public gathering places, such as Plato's Academy and Aristotle's Lyceum. It was not until the conquests of Alexander the Great, however, that Greek aristocrats, inspired by the extraordinary descriptions brought back

from his campaigns, started to systematically emulate the pleasure gardens, or *paradeisos*, of Persia and the East. The 4th-century BC philosopher Epicurus (whose pleasure-loving life-style prompted the term "epicurean") bequeathed his lavish garden to the city of Athens as a public park. Public gardens with fountains and grottoes began appearing in Greek cities and colonies. Fountains and statuary graced private gardens where favorite plantings included not only roses, irises, lilies, violets, and herbs, but small fruit and nut trees. No known description of Epicurus's garden survives, but in all likelihood that is where luxury in the western garden first appeared. Centuries later Voltaire described in a letter (1755) his own "delicious" retreat near Geneva as "the palace of a philosopher with the gardens of Epicurus."

The Sources of Roman Gardens

But it was the Romans who provided the model for the western landscaping tradition; the gardens they created were to leave a lasting impression on the history of garden design. Their earliest endeavors, however, were quite humble; the *hortus,* a herb, fruit, or vegetable plot, was, like the young Republic, strictly practical. But by the end

The integration of garden and villa within a landscape was perhaps ancient Rome's greatest contribution to the art of landscape design. This concept, illustrated in a reconstruction of the Emperor Tiberius's opulent villa at Capri (left), was copied in Renaissance gardens.

The Greeks had a naturalistic approach to gardening; their sacred groves, dedicated to gods, were selected because they were naturally beautiful spots and did not need dressing up. Planting was confined

of the 2nd century BC a vogue for the more luxuriant art and architecture of Greece had taken hold and the refinements of the Hellenistic period (323–150 BC) could be seen in the art of garden-making in and around Rome. The Romans looked to the East, as well, for inspiration; but rather than slavishly imitating Greek, Egyptian, or Persian antecedents, they combined all three into a sophisticated hybrid aesthetic.

The concept of the "pleasure garden" began to emerge from the *hortus*. The Romans appropriated the central pool of Egyptian gardens and, where space permitted,

to urban gathering places, such as agoras, temple precincts, and promenades. Cemeteries, originally simply ornamented with asphodel and acanthus plants, were transformed into full-blown funerary gardens. Auguste Leloir's painting of Homer (1841) evokes the Greek predilection for natural settings.

adopted an ornamental "canal." Water—gushing and gurgling from fountains, pools, and cascades—came to be a hallmark of the Roman garden and provided a welcome retreat during scorching summer months. The use of evergreens (often curiously shaped into "topiaries") and statuary also became dominant features of Roman gardens. This new tradition, however, was not approved by all; in his practical handbook *De Agri Cultura* (2nd century BC), the statesman and "agronomist" Marcus Porcius Cato condemned the unbridled decorativeness of contemporary gardens.

Much of what we know about Roman gardens was learned from the wall paintings of Pompeii. These delightful trompe l'oeil murals, buried for centuries beneath volcanic ash, show the Roman passion for greenery and allowed the garden vista to extend beyond the limited confines of the home.

Town and Country Gardens

Urban Romans tended gardens both within the courtyards of their town houses and behind them. In both
cases, the garden was an extension of the home, linked
to it by colonnaded walkways or paths. A spate of
horticultural treatises in the 1st century
BC encouraged the development of
more opulent gardens around country
villas, which doubled as working
farms. These botanical texts by Lucius
Junius Moderatus Columella, Marcus
Terentius Varro, and even Virgil (as
in his masterly *Georgics*) would later
inspire the humanists during
the Renaissance.

In his treatise *De Re Rustica* (1st
century BC) Varro mocked the
architectural pretensions of country estates that were
considered incomplete without such Greek elements as a
peristylon (colonnade), *peripteros* (pergola), and *ornithron*
(aviary), although his own garden, in fact, featured an
ornithron that not only sheltered nightingales, thrushes,
and other songbirds, but doubled as a dining room
featuring a revolving table, and hot- and cold-water taps.

Late in the 1st century AD, Pliny the Younger laid down
the essentials of the Roman garden in his letters describing his own beloved gardens: A garden must be sited to
take full advantage of sun, view, and cool breezes, and it
must be so linked to the villa by colonnades, courtyards,
and porticoes that villa and garden are inseparable.

The Pompeian garden
provides a model in
miniature of traditional
Roman design. The
colonnaded terrace of the
courtyard, or peristyle,
was often lined with

elaborate wall paintings
(such as the one at the top
of the page). The garden
itself would have been
embellished with cheerful
fountains, architectural
trellises draped with vines
(*treillage*), small trees,
shrubbery, and flowers.
Romans loved water, and
decorative canals (above)
were common features of
Pompeian gardens.

The Epitome of Roman Splendor: Hadrian's Villa

By the early Empire the contrived "natural" look of Pliny's day had blossomed into sophisticated splendor. Cicero's villa at Tusculum already boasted an academy and lyceum, but for sheer opulence nothing could compare with the villa the Emperor Hadrian built at Tivoli between AD 118 and 138, the year he died. Tivoli took full advantage of the undulating terrain: Most of the buildings are nestled in sheltering natural basins, while the terraces command views of the surrounding countryside. And although scattered over hundreds of acres, gardens and garden structures are linked by common axes. The Romans' dual tendency—their need for intimacy and urge to dominate space—reflects the ethos of a conquering people, as bent on safe-guarding their civilization as they were on imposing it.

Hadrian's sprawling extravaganza of buildings and monuments just below the Tiburtine hills was a fanciful recreation of famous buildings and sites the emperor had seen during his travels throughout the Empire, among them the Vale of Tempe in Thessaly and the Stoa Poikile of Athens. A reflecting pool (below) was modeled on the Canopus canal, a branch of the Nile delta. The garden ruins served as blueprints for landscape architects of the Renaissance.

The Influence of Persia and Islam

The palace complex of Cyrus the Great (ruled 558–529 BC) at Pasargadae was but one of the many royal parks—mirrors of paradise—in Persia. The open, four-sided, geometric structures between the Audience Hall and Private Palace featured water channels cut into the rock and small square cultivated plots with trees, shrubs, and plants. Garden pavilions served as vantage points from which the ruler enjoyed a sweeping view of the natural landscape and, symbolically, the people he controlled. The Persian prince Cyrus the Younger (424–401 BC) personally laid out most of his "paradise garden," oversaw its construction, and even worked alongside his gardeners. The Greek historian Xenophon described the eastern gardens that he saw during the Persian Wars as places of beautiful plantings, carefully spaced trees, and delightfully exquisite smells.

Heir to Persian gardens, the garden tradition of Islam took root in the 8th century AD and eventually spread into Asia, Africa, and part of Europe, wherever the followers of Mohammed (c. 570–632) ventured in their pursuit of conquest.

The seaside villa appearing in this wall painting from the House of Marcus Lucretius near Pompeii follows the general tenets of Roman garden design: Villa and garden should be carefully positioned to take full advantage of the larger natural landscape (in this case, Vesuvius looming in the background and views of the water from the front); and the architecture should be integrated into the "borrowed scenery" beyond the space of the actual garden. To ensure divine protection, property lines were demarcated by herms —stone boundary posts surmounted by carved heads of Hermes. Romans developed a passion for clipping box and other greenery into inconceivable shapes, which came to be called topiary.

When the Arab hordes overran the old Persian Empire late in the 7th century, these nomads on horseback or camelback discovered the garden paradise that the Prophet had promised to a people who had to contend with the harsh realities of desert life. Here was the earthly equivalent of the luxuriant, verdant Heavenly Paradise, described in the Koran as a place of "spreading shade," with "fountains of gushing water," and abundant "fruits, palm trees, and pomegranates." Muslims considered the garden a universal symbol of life and hope. Not surprisingly, green became the emblematic color of Islam.

Four Sacred Elements and a Symbolic Geometry

The symbolic importance of the number four, which was to be such a key element of the Islamic garden is, in fact, far older than Islam; its very ancient genealogy includes the sacred elements of water, fire, air, and earth. "And a river went out of Eden to water the garden," the Book of Genesis tells us, "and from there it parted and became four riverheads." The ancient Persians believed that a cross divided the universe into four quarters and that a spring of life lay at its center; Mesopotamian hunting preserves were likewise divided into four with a building in the middle. In Buddhist iconography, four rivers branching from a common source symbolize fertility and timelessness. From these sources

Islamic gardens symbolized Allah's promise of heavenly reward as described in the Koran. As in Persia, allegorical meaning informed every element of a garden, including the trees: cypresses, for example, represented eternity.

The scene depicted in this 16th-century Persian miniature (left) is part of an ancient genealogy that reaches back more than ten centuries to the Persian king and gardener Cyrus the Younger. In the parched Middle East, a garden was considered more than an oasis of delight—it was a sign of superior culture. The Mogul emperors had a real passion for gardening. As a young man, Babur, future invader of India (ruled 1526–30), lived in Samarkand amid Persian-style irrigated orchards and gardens. His memoirs include detailed descriptions of the gardens he himself laid out. Here the emperor is seen supervising a cohort of gardeners. Intersecting irrigation channels divide the enclosure into four raised geometric flower and plant beds, forming the traditional quadripartite pattern repeated in Persian garden carpets (above).

evolved the *chahar bagh*, or literally "fourfold garden," the basis of the Islamic courtyard with its centrally positioned fountain or pool. Such courtyards were laid out in buildings both secular (private dwellings, palaces, bazaars) and religious (mosques and *madrasas*, or theological colleges). This plan expressed unity, order, and the serenity of an enclosed space focused on the divine gift of water.

The traditional Islamic garden was rectangular and surrounded by a wall, but trees and low plantings

softened its strict geometry. Like the Greeks and Romans, Arabs were sensitive to the pervading spirit peculiar to a location, and their gardens are remarkably diverse despite architectural constraints. This garden tradition became so deeply rooted that it was adopted by Islamic converts as far-flung as the Moguls in India and the Moors in North Africa and Spain.

The Moorish Gardens of Spain

Islamic gardens first appeared in Europe in the 8th century, when the Arabs conquered southern and north-eastern Spain. Abd ar-Rahman I fled Damascus, settled in Andalusia, and became the first independent emir of Cordova (ruled 756–88). When Abd ar-Rahman III, the first of the western caliphs, came to power (ruled 912–61), he immediately began laying out a large garden at Medina Azahara.

The Muslim conquerors did more than create beautiful pleasure gardens; they brought with them the Greek botanical texts that had been collected and translated in Baghdad starting around 830. By the 10th century, thousands of private gardens dotted the countryside

In the splendid gardens and courtyards of the Alhambra (above) and the Generalife (opposite), both in Granada, in southern Spain, paths or water channels intersect at centrally located pools, basins, or pavilions; thus, all views from these focal points terminate at an architectural element. The designs are geometric, but perfectly adapted to the *genius loci*, or unique spirit of the place. Islamic gardens are water gardens, and the pervasive presence of gurgling, running, spurting, or motionless water signifies its importance as a symbol of purity and of life itself.

A 14th-century French miniature of the sultan of Cordova in his garden (left) testifies to the cultural exchange between the Islamic world and Christendom during the Middle Ages.

around Cordova, and
an efficient irrigation system
for growing food crops was in place.
The gardens of Andalusia were reportedly
filled with the scent of flowers, singing birds,
and the whirring of waterwheels. The 11th-
century Patio de los Naranjos (Court of the Orange
Trees) in Cordova, its rows of orange trees aligned
with columns inside the mosque, remains to this
day the purest expression of the garden of the
great Muslim Umayyad dynasty.

Moorish influence persisted in Spain long
after the fall of Seville and Cordova in the 13th
century. The gardens of the last remaining Muslim
stronghold of Granada were set on steep hillsides
overlooking the city. Most sumptuous of all
Moorish gardens, the Alhambra and the
Generalife, embody the Islamic

A small private Persian garden (left): cool, orderly, geometrical, focused on water. Cypresses, symbols of eternity, and Oriental planes—the quintessential shade tree—hug the high enclosing wall. Dioscorides, a 1st-century AD Greek army doctor, pioneered the description of plants and their healing properties in his book *De Materia Medica*. The Arabs initially relied on classical botanical literature but went on to become accomplished observers and investigators in their own right during the Middle Ages and produced numerous manuscripts on botany (below left).

vision of the garden as an earthly paradise. They are a precious part of Europe's cultural heritage and rank among the loveliest gardens anywhere on earth. Though much altered, they are the only surviving gardens in Europe dating from the 13th and 14th centuries. For sheer beauty they rival the splendid gardens of Mogul India.

The Enduring Influence of Islamic Scholarship

The Arabs translated and dutifully preserved the scientific legacy of ancient Greece. The Baghdad caliph Harun ar-Rashid and his successors imported exotic plants and seeds from Asia and Africa. Despite enmity and warfare between Muslim and Christian, the classical botanical literature they rescued worked its way into medieval Europe, where an awakening appreciation for the sensual delights already

familiar to the Islamic world gave fresh impetus to the concept of the pleasure garden. The popular "flowery mead" (or meadow), for example, is a restrained variation on the Arab practice of sowing seeds of different flowers within the same plot. Both civilizations delighted in fragrances and indulged their passion for roses. Arab influence was revolutionary in other respects: By the 13th century, a botanical garden had been established at the medical school in Montpellier, France, and the eminent botanist Ibn ar-Baytar of Malaga had classified some fourteen thousand plants in his *Pharmacopoeia*. The Arabs led the field not only in the preservation of ancient botanical learning, but in plant collecting, identification, and research. Their legacy has become an integral part of Western culture.

Arab expertise in hydraulic engineering is evident in this diagram (below) of a pumping system from a book of mechanical devices.

Monasteries kept utilitarian gardening alive during the Middle Ages, the centuries-long bridge between the collapse of the Roman Empire and the Renaissance. The Church appropriated the symbolism of the walled *hortus conclusus* (enclosed garden), while aristocrats and poets embraced the secular garden paradise of the *hortus deliciarum* (garden of delight). In these two metaphors lies the essence of the medieval garden.

CHAPTER II

THE MEDIEVAL GARDEN

The earliest realistic representations of medieval gardens, like this 15th-century Flemish painting of a pleasure orchard during a feast (opposite), feature pavilions, turf seats, ornamental trees, and, of course, flowers. To the right is a botanical detail from a French manuscript.

The Shadow of the Dark Ages

When the last Roman emperor was deposed at Ravenna

in 476, political and economic unease settled over Europe. Faced with successive waves of invaders, people secured themselves behind the heavy doors of moated castles or within fortified hilltop towns, leaving little space for the cultivation of gardens. Apollinarius Sidonius, a 5th-century Gallo-Roman aristocrat who became the bishop of Clermont around 470, was the last to describe a Roman garden; but his lakeside country retreat in the Auvergne was considerably smaller than Pliny the Younger's. Another three centuries were to elapse before Charlemagne (ruled 800–14), attempting to revive the dying art of gardening, ordered in his *Decree Concerning Towns* that each town "in all Crown lands" plant a garden with seventy-three herbs and sixteen fruit and nut trees. In the interim, the art of garden-making had sustained an

One might gather from the bucolic scenes depicted in this 4th-century Carthaginian mosaic (above) that bountiful harvests, the art of garden-making, and refined country pleasures continued to be a way of life in the former colonies of the Roman Empire. In fact, the early Middle Ages witnessed a cultural regression in Europe that spared neither agriculture nor aesthetic horticulture. Had it not been for monastic communities and practical gardeners, the grafting of fruit trees —artificially attaching a limb from one tree onto another, shown in the Gallo-Roman mosaic at the left—and other techniques might not have survived.

During the Middle Ages, monasteries played a pivotal role in preserving the arts and sciences, including kitchen and physic—or medicinal—gardening skills. Their libraries were repositories of classical garden literature. As we can see in the engraving below, monks cultivated subsistence gardens with their own hands and by the sweat of their own brows. Their genuine feeling for nature was nurtured by their traditional belief in the biblical Garden of Eden. Tending these earthly equivalents of paradise lost—and promised— provided food for the soul as well as the body. The *Liber de Cultura Hortorum*, commonly known as the *Hortulus* or "Little Garden," was a poem written in the 9th century by Swiss monk Walafrid Strabo, whose observations on the gardener's peaceful but demanding life are as touching as they are evocative. Come spring, what should be done about the stinging nettles: *Quid facerum?* All he could do with the offensive roots was tear them out.

appalling loss. Master gardeners in the employ of noblemen, churchmen, and sovereigns kept practical knowledge from disappearing altogether by passing on their horticultural skills and techniques to their apprentices. The garden tradition was thus preserved, but for several centuries was largely reduced to subsistence gardening. The gardens that remained took on a new character; they were walled in and protected from the danger and uncertainty that spread across Europe once it had lost the stability of the Roman Empire.

Subdividing gardens into neat geometric plots, shown here (left) in the Italian lawyer Pietro de' Crescenzi's most influential agricultural text *Opus Ruralium Commodorum* (c. 1305), was the basis of all future formal European gardens.

Carolingian Gardening and Agriculture

The earliest documentary evidence of medieval gardens dates from the Carolingian empire. The powerful heads of great abbeys served as Charlemagne's advisers on gardening. Abbot Benedict of Aniane in Languedoc is known to have corresponded with his colleagues in Germany and England and exchanged medicinal plants with Alcuin of York around the year 800. As they continued to share what information they had, churchmen emerged as the real custodians of horticultural learning and formed a link, however tenuous, between past and present. At the same time, despite centuries of barbarian invasions, contact with the Islamic world encouraged the migration of ideas and plants from Spain and the East.

In addition to Charlemagne's list, a detailed

9th-century plan for an ideal Benedictine monastery at St. Gall, Switzerland, survives. It shows three types of gardens within the monastery walls: a physic garden of medicinal herbs next to the infirmary; a kitchen garden with narrow strip beds for lettuce, onions, beets, carrots, and aromatics; and a cemetery with espaliered (trained to grow along a trellis) fruit and nut trees. Roses, irises, and lilies would have been cultivated in these utilitarian gardens for their fragrance and religious symbolism. All the

During the Middle Ages, plants were treasured not only for their healing powers, but for the sensual delight they afforded in such luxury products as perfumes and cosmetics. This miniature from a *Tacuinum Sanitatis* or "Table of Health" (left), a popular botanical study focusing on the medicinal properties of plants, shows women making scented water from rose petals. Every monastery had a physic garden of medicinal herbs; priests cultivated flowers, fruit trees, and vegetables

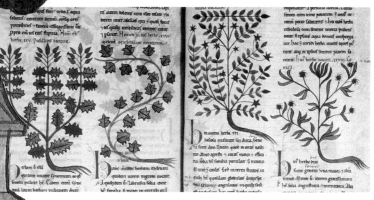

species noted in this plan for the ideal monastic garden are included in Charlemagne's list.

From the St. Gall plan, Charlemagne's garden decree, a poem by the monk Walafrid Strabo, and a gardener's calendar indicating month-by-month garden chores by another monk, Wandelbert of Prüm, we can piece together a reasonably complete picture of practical and aesthetic gardening techniques during this period.

alongside the medicinal plants in their garden plots. (An unruly vine creeps out over the roof of a monastic garden, center.) Botanical treatises based on Arab scholarship, such as the one shown above, circulated widely throughout Europe.

The Secular Garden

The three garden types illustrated in the plan from St. Gall could also be found, with modifications, outside the walls of the monastery. In place of the cemetery garden, however, we see gradual evidence of pleasure gardens. These gardens designed for delight became quite varied. Providing a warmth and intimacy lacking within the walls of a stone castle, they could be appreciated either from

The trellises in medieval gardens were far less elaborate than the generous expanses of latticework fences to be found in Roman gardens, but were nonetheless a recurring theme in the *hortus conclusus*, or "enclosed garden" of the Middle Ages. The garden pictured in one 15th-century miniature (inset opposite) is circumscribed by palings and woven willow, but enclosures could also be fashioned from stone walls, dense hedges, or clipped trees. All gardens, orchards, and hunting preserves were shielded from the pervasive insecurity of the times, but not at the expense of the imagination. To the left is an ornamental pool stocked with fish and below, an illustration from a book of health (or *Tacuinum Sanitatis*) shows a mandrake plant, believed to cause insanity, sending a terror-stricken farmer running for his life.

above, through the windows of the home, or at garden level. There were two basic types of pleasure garden. The square or oblong flowering garden was enclosed by trellis fencing and featured a lawn, crisscrossed paths, a fountain, raised flower beds, and sometimes fruit trees. Occasionally one might find a checkerboard pattern alternating turf with greenery, or shrubs clipped into unusual shapes. The second type, the *viridarium*, or ornamental orchard, provided not only elegant displays of evergreens and fruit trees but shade for strolling, often by a pond or lake.

The medieval gardens that later inspired the more elaborate botanical gardens of the Renaissance were rooted in Islamic learning. Founded by Arab physicians from Spain, the renowned medical school of Montpellier, a possession of the kings of Aragon from 1202 to 1349, already had a physic garden by around 1250.

The First Public Promenades and Parks

Charlemagne's decree included the planting of

public pleasure gardens. He himself had lavish "pleasure parks" featuring peacocks and animals, as well as elaborate vineyards for wine production. This practice must have been widespread, for such parks or "meadows"—*pratum* in Latin—are known to have existed in Madrid (Prado), Vienna (Prater), and Paris (Le-Pré-aux-Clercs, Saint-Germain-des-Prés) by the year 1000. Until recently it was thought that there was no such thing as a landscaped park before the Renaissance. We now know that much earlier, the Arab interpretation of the enclosed Persian "paradise" had reached northern Europe by way of Sicily and Italy and that Norman forays into Calabria and Sicily helped spread it west to England.

There was a constant emphasis in the medieval garden on geometry and containment, a taming of the wilderness that lay beyond; this tendency was manifested in tunneled arbors, or trees shaped into tunnels, and in the elaborate walls and trellises shown in garden illustrations of the period. Even the plant beds, usually raised slightly from the ground, were carefully compartmentalized.

The *Hortus Conclusus* as Christian Allegory

The powerful religious symbolism of the *hortus conclusus,* "garden enclosed" or secret garden within a garden, was inspired by the description of the beloved in the Song of Solomon: "A garden enclosed is my sister, my spouse; a spring shut up, a fountain sealed. Thy plants are an orchard of pomegranates, with pleasant fruits: spikenard and saffron, calamus and cinnamon, with all trees of frankincense;

Gardens reflect the duality of sacred and secular life during the Middle Ages. The "Mary Garden" was a religious allegory in which every flower had symbolic meaning (above). The literary garden was a trysting place, the idealized setting for romantic love as formulated in *Le Roman de la Rose* (left). Both were imaginary, but they mirrored real-life gardens.

myrrh and aloes, with all the chief spices." This figurative garden became a visual allegory for the purity of the Virgin Mary. A veritable cult surrounding Mary arose during the Middle Ages and led to the creation of "Mary Gardens" in which each flower was assigned a specific meaning. Of all the flowers that became symbols of virtue in these metaphorical gardens of purity,

Lady Nature holds the key to the Garden of Desire in this manuscript painting from the High Middle Ages.

The "Mary Garden" painted by an unknown Rhenish master in the early 15th century is at once an exemplary *hortus conclusus* and a telling record of late medieval gardening practices. The mingling of trees and plants both along the walls and in the grass is, in fact, a reinterpretation of the naturalistic sacred grove of classical antiquity, walled off from the outside world and converted to Christianity. The Virgin Mary is surrounded by angels, saints, and a chorus of songbirds. The saints perform ritual tasks: Saint Dorothy is picking cherries. At least eighteen kinds of flowers can be identified, including Madonna lily, flag iris, cowslip, lily-of-the-valley, daisy, hollyhock, peony, and spring snowflake, as well as strawberries in flower and fruit. The Mary Garden was the religious counterpart to the secular courtly garden of the later Middle Ages—a place for socializing and relaxing.

none was more important than one identified with the Virgin herself: the rose.

Hortus Deliciarum: **The Literary Garden**

Gardens of another kind—the imaginary gardens of literature, paintings, and illuminated manuscripts—thrived during the Middle Ages. The enchanted garden

in the verse romance *Erec et Enide* by Chrétien de Troyes (c. 1168) is a paradise of gentle birdsong and eternally fresh fruit and flowers. Begun around 1230 by Guillaume de Lorris and completed in 1280 in a more satiric vein by Jean de Meun, *Le Roman de la Rose*, a manual of courtly love, proved extraordinarily influential and was translated into English by Chaucer a century later. In it, the hero falls in love with a most beautiful rosebud.

These allegorical, Edenesque dreamworlds were, in fact, hybrid creations that grafted an idealized garden onto gardens as they actually existed. In chivalric literature, Christian symbols were transformed into personifications of love, beauty, and other earthly delights.

First Glimmers of the Renaissance

In the middle of the 14th century, the Italian poet
Giovanni Boccaccio provided a link between the medieval
garden and the splendors to come in his collection of one
hundred tales, the *Decameron*. In it, a group of Florentine
aristocrats seeking refuge from the plague finds sanctuary
in Fiesole, a town in the nearby hills above the city and
rediscovers the refined pleasures of civilized living.
Although the gardens of this country retreat are
medieval in layout, their sophistication heralds the spirit
of the magnificent villa gardens of the Renaissance.

The 15th-century king and passionate gardener
René of Anjou (ruled 1435–42) inherited the kingdom
of Naples and Sicily. He took a lively interest in
agronomy and viticulture and is credited with
introducing the Muscat vine and the mulberry to
France. The gardens that he planted everywhere have
long since disappeared, but the reputation of "good
king René" lives on in popular mythology and in
literary works that highlight landscape and pastoral
themes. René's best-known work is *Le Livre du Coeur
d'Amour Epris* (*The Book of the Love-Smitten Heart*) a
treatise on profane love, which, though modeled on
contemporary romances, demonstrates remarkable
poetic sensitivity to landscape settings.

One of the gardens
in Boccaccio's
Decameron—the Valley
of the Ladies—is still a
medieval blend of the
natural and the artificial:
a circular, flower-studded
lawn surrounded by
symmetrical hills. But the
introduction to the Third
Day describes a walled
garden (left) with a lawn
and a "fountain of pure
white marble." A statue
at the fountain's center
spurts water that
eventually reappears in
"cleverly wrought little
channels"; the elaborate
art of hydraulics was to
be perfected in the
Renaissance. Opposite
left: René of Anjou in a
room with windows
looking onto an elegant
garden. Two other
medieval manuscripts
depict the utilitarian and
recreational aspects of
gardens: fruit gathering
and archery.

Like the ancients before him, the 14th-century Italian poet Petrarch considered the garden an ideal setting for instruction, introspection, and poetry. The one he laid out in the Euganean Hills in the north of Italy did not quite recreate the classical precedents it emulated, but it helped pave the way for the rebirth of garden art. The Italian humanists of the Renaissance yearned to recapture the aesthetic and intellectual ideals of the classical world.

CHAPTER III

THE GARDENS OF RENAISSANCE ITALY

Artist and art historian Giorgio Vasari described Villa Medici at Castello, near Florence, as "the most rich, magnificent, and ornamental garden in Europe" (right). It was divided into clearly delineated and distinctive spatial units, like the Mantuan garden opposite, while the overall plan was organized along an upwardly sloping central axis. The garden had become an extension of the villa and, for the first time since the end of the Roman Empire, opened confidently to the world beyond.

Alberti and the Classical Theory of Proportion

Gardens played an important part in the lives of the ancient Greek and Roman philosophers, poets, politicians, and cultured aristocrats whom the humanists of Renaissance Italy held up as models. Lorenzo de' Medici's Giardino di San Marco was a retreat and workplace for sculptors (including a young Michelangelo), while the Medici villa and gardens at Careggi served as a meeting place for the Platonic Academy and was the birthplace of the humanist movement. Both were inspired by the writings of the 15th-century Florentine architect and scholar Leon Battista Alberti, who relied upon the authority of the ancients, such as Pliny the Younger and Vitruvius, and reaffirmed their conviction that beauty of form results when all parts are proportionate to the whole.

In his treatise *De Re Aedificatoria* (printed 1485), Alberti notes that the ideal country estate is a place where one can enjoy to the fullest all the pleasures nature has to offer, a place conducive to contemplation. Drawing on

Tuscan villas were modeled on classically inspired villa designs recommended by Leon Battista Alberti, epitome of the versatile "Renaissance man." Their gardens were laid out along a straight axis from the villa and punctuated by tree-lined paths, or *allées*, and pergolas covered with climbing shrubs or vines. In these settings one could enjoy all the pleasures and diversions of civilized living, including philosophical discussion (above). Opposite below: The Pitti Palace, Florence, as it looked in the 16th century.

descriptions of Roman villa gardens, he
recommended the use of box topiary, and
hillside sites that command magnificent views.
A garden still had to be walled, but its location
on sloping terrain should draw one's attention
from the area immediately around the house to
the distant view beyond. Ideally, villa, garden,
and site should form a harmonious whole.

Rome and the Renaissance Garden

Florence paved the way for the rebirth of
garden art, but the real impetus came from
Rome. Florence provided the conceptual framework:
the emphasis on architecture, subordination of plants to
overall design, and heavy use of evergreens, all of which
were to become hallmarks of Italian gardens until the end
of the 18th century. But it was in and around Rome that
these concepts were to be embraced, fully developed, and
perpetuated. Garden-making there was stimulated early
on by the *villeggiatura*, or country homes—the custom
of retreating to a place in the country dated back to
Roman times—and by the villa's growing importance
as a center of social
activity outside the city.
The home was no

H *ypnerotomachia
Poliphili* (*Dream of
Poliphilus*, c. 1499), an
allegorical dream-
romance by Francesco
Colonna, is a distillation
of the literary sources of
the Renaissance. Its
woodcut illustrations
(above) had a profound
influence on Renaissance
landscape designs.

longer strictly a medieval fortress but a pleasant rural retreat from the city. Crenellated facades were transformed into more welcoming structures; moats became ornamental fishponds; and the enclosed garden "rooms" of the Middle Ages developed into substantial architectural elements in their own right, linking the house to the surrounding countryside, rather than just extending the walls of the house.

Rome lay in ruins when Pope Martin V (ruled 1417–31) entered the city on 30 September 1420, thus bringing peace to the papacy and an end to the era of Avignon's preeminence. Several decades were to pass before Rome emerged from desolation. The first great cultured Quattrocento pope, Nicholas V (ruled 1447–55), had come into contact with humanist circles during his frequent stays in Florence. Under their influence the papal court became a beacon of scholarship; Nicholas V was to found the Vatican library. This period also witnessed the rediscovery of the "antiquities" of ancient Rome and a newfound appreciation of their educational and inspirational value.

Formal terrace gardens carved out of the slopes of Monte Mario lead to the entrance of Villa Madama's *giardino segreto* (above). Inspired by Pliny the Younger's description of his own seaside retreat, Raphael's master plan for the gardens, though never completed, had far-reaching effects on garden design around Rome— foremost among these was the interpenetration of villa and garden.

Popes, Cardinals, Patrons, and Master Architects

Even before ascending the papal throne,

Pope Julius II (ruled 1503–13), who was to become one of the outstanding builders of Rome, had decided on a garden setting (since partially destroyed) for his extensive collection of antique sculpture, most famously what is known as the *Apollo Belvedere*. When he moved his treasures to the nearby Villa Belvedere, he envisioned a huge garden space that would link the villa with the existing palace of the Vatican and provide a suitable backdrop both for his sculptures and for the grand ceremonies of a papal court. The person he chose for this project was Donato Bramante, whose ingenious system of rising terraces, which were linked by stairs and ramps embodying the Renaissance preoccupation with perspective, culminated at the top with a large semi-circular apse. From this moment on, the garden became a primary concern of the architects of the Renaissance.

The first great Roman suburban retreat of the Renaissance was Villa Madama. Probably inspired by the Medici family estate at Fiesole, it was designed by Raphael, Giulio Romano, and Giovanni da Udine and built for the Tuscan cardinal Giulio de' Medici between 1516 and 1520 as a loose interpretation of a classical Roman villa. The site was carved out of a hillside to capture a breathtaking view of Rome. A recognition of the larger landscape informs the majestic plan, which is founded upon the relationship of

Below: Inspired by classical Roman precedent, the immense Belvedere Court of the Vatican is divided into three terrace levels that create the effect of a gigantic outdoor theater within an architectural landscape. A connecting series of stairways and ramps, which climaxed at an apse, afforded the terraces nearest the papal apartments a magnificent view. The middle terrace served as a viewing platform overlooking the arena space below. Laid out as a formal garden, the upper terrace (nearest the old Villa Belvedere) served as an open-air sculpture museum.

architecture to site. This unfinished masterpiece was to influence later villa gardens.

Villa d'Este

The gardens of Villa d'Este at Tivoli, overlooking the golden Campagna di Roma, are undoubtedly the most spectacular of all Renaissance gardens. Begun in 1550 for Cardinal Ippolito II d'Este and completed thirty years later, they were designed by the architect and antiquarian Pirro Ligorio. He combined a thorough grasp of classical sources with a brilliant imagination to create an original garden design which, though inspired by Hadrian's Villa nearby, was entirely his own. Originally the entrance to the garden was at the lowest level, where visitors could take in the full sweep of the overall layout. After making their way from one marvel-studded level to the next, they ended up at the house and there were treated to an astounding view of the countryside. Villa d'Este is the consummate water garden of Europe. The statuary, much of it pillaged from Hadrian's Villa, has since disappeared, as have the water-powered performing statuary and amusing water games. The fountains, however, are as magical as ever.

The *Giardino Segreto*

By now the stately splendor of Rome's Renaissance gardens had little in common with Alberti's rural ideal of "a retreat near town where a man is at liberty to do just as he pleases," except for one curious holdover from the Middle Ages: the *giardino segreto*, or secret garden,

Villa d'Este crowns a series of terraces that are linked by a dramatic axial stairway and flanked by adjoining ramps with low hedge borders of laurel, box, and yew. Water is its primary element and unifying theme: Nowhere else are so many cascades, fountains, and basins deployed to such dramatic, imaginative, and ingenious effect. The enchanting Pathway of a Hundred Fountains (left) consists of three rows of small fountains punctuated by stucco reliefs of scenes from Ovid's *Metamorphoses*. Water gushes, falls, flows, gurgles, and sparkles in the sunlight.

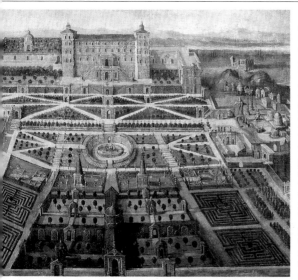

Although it is difficult to pinpoint the contributions patrons, architects, and sculptors made to 16th-century Italian garden design, one must single out the Medici and Este families and two individuals: Pirro Ligorio, who orchestrated the symphony of water at Villa d'Este, and Giacomo Barozzi da Vignola, the greatest landscape architect and theorist of the Renaissance. In 1556 Cardinal Alessandro Farnese commissioned Vignola to transform a pentagonal fortress at Caprarola into a palace, eventually spurring the cardinal's rival, Ippolito II d'Este, to sink a fortune into his own gardens at Tivoli (above). The exquisite *giardino segreto* at Caprarola (below) was designed as a hideaway for a Renaissance prince.

descendant of the medieval *hortus conclusus*. Whether tiny (Villa Lante), tucked away behind a grotto (Villa Giulia, Rome), or sublimely beautiful (Palazzo Farnese, Caprarola), the "secret" garden provided a haven of tranquillity secluded from the vast expanses and sweeping vistas of the rest of the garden beyond. Designed by Giacomo Barozzi da Vignola, the *giardino segreto* at Caprarola is separated from the palazzo by dense woods and surrounds a pleasure pavilion, or casino, overlooking a "water chain" sculpted in stone. Rows of stone statues with urns on their heads keep watch over the garden on three sides.

Villa Lante at Bagnaia

The garden of Villa Lante at Bagnaia is attributed to Vignola, who designed the Farnese gardens at Caprarola twenty miles away and worked with Vasari at Villa Giulia in Rome. More than just a great architect, Vignola successfully transposed and adapted his theory of dramatic spatial composition to the world of gardens.

Villa Lante marked the first time architecture took second place

to an overall garden design. The relationship between the formal terraces of the garden and the surrounding wild woods, or *bosco,* was totally unprecedented (the *bosco* had often been near to, but always separate from, the formal garden) and would be taken a step further by Baroque landscape designers. It was also the first time since

Water cascades down a long chain from a basin flanked by two giants in the Farnese gardens at Caprarola (below). A stone "water chain" also forms part of the central axis of nearby Villa Lante at Bagnaia (opposite above and below), with all probability, also designed by Vignola. This is a perfect Renaissance garden—nature and architecture are harmoniously balanced; the buildings defer to the garden landscape and its allegorical meaning in a composition that shows the inspired architect at the height of his powers.

antiquity that the iconography of a European garden embraced the blatantly pagan forces of nature: a statue of Pegasus, surrounded by water nymphs stands just beyond the entrance; cascades flow down from the woods over hoary water gods.

Above all, however, this Renaissance garden is a wonderful display of stone and water. The general theme of the garden, the loveliest and best preserved of any from this period, suggests a path of discovery leading from a mysterious, mythic Golden Age to the cultivated elegance of the Renaissance—a metaphor translated into the language of water that is perfectly still one moment and bubbling the next.

Water from a hillside spring flows down cascades and water chains at Villa Lante, swirling and gurgling through fountains of dolphins, giants, and candles, before making its final descent toward the square water terrace and Fountain of the Moors (below).

Labyrinthine Hedges

Mazes reach back to antiquity, to the legend of the half-man–half-bull Minotaur that King Minos confined in the labyrinth beneath his palace. The labyrinth appears as a decorative motif in Roman mosaics and frescoes, and Christians used it to symbolize the arduous path to Jerusalem and, allegorically, salvation. These mazes were set in the stone pavements of churches and, in medieval England, cut in turf.

The raised hedge maze of clipped yew, box, or privet is a Renaissance creation: Alberti mistakenly believed this type of geometric composition to have been a feature of classical Roman gardens. In any event, mazes were commonly found in Italy by the early 15th century; the Villa d'Este at Tivoli had at least four. Meanwhile, knot gardens (interlaced bands of clipped shrubbery around beds of flowers or herbs) were being laid out in England. In France, Leonardo da Vinci made a note to himself that King Francis I's maze was in need of repair; and drawings of mazes fill Jacques Androuet du Cerceau's treatise *Les Plus Excellents Bâtiments de France* (1576). Sixteenth-century mazes were still only knee-high, but by the 17th

The "knots" typical of 16th-century French and English gardens featured intricate designs fashioned from continuous interlacing bands of greenery (above left). Like hedge mazes (below), they symbolized infinity. The French writer François Rabelais mentions that the "beautiful garden of delight" in the Abbey of Thélème had a "handsome labyrinth." In England, mazes were bewildering outdoor theaters of choice and chance where tall hedges shielded lovers from view as they indulged in amorous pursuit.

century they towered over visitors (as at Hampton Court Palace, or the maze designed for Versailles in 1667 by Charles Perrault, reteller of such fairy tales as "Sleeping Beauty" and "Little Red Riding Hood").

Giochi d'Acqua: **Humor in the Garden**

The *giochi d'acqua*—hidden water jets that delighted 17th- and 18th-century travelers in Italy—brought classical or commonplace subjects to life by means of sophisticated hydraulic devices. Unsuspecting visitors would trip a mechanism and end up drenched with water or standing before performing statuary. Such "water tricks" were not unknown during the Middle Ages, a legacy of Arab improvements on mechanical devices invented by Hero of Alexandria in the 1st century AD. The Owl Fountain at Villa d'Este—a group of birds that sang by water pressure and fell silent whenever a mechanical owl turned towards them—has been traced to Hero's *Pneumatica*, as have many other *giochi d'acqua* throughout Europe, including Hellbrunn in Austria and Wilton House in England.

Hortus Medicus: **The First Botanical Gardens**

Garden design in Florence, Rome, or for that matter anywhere else in Italy did not revolve around planting

Already popular during the Middle Ages, *giochi d'acqua*—water tricks or games—were as fashionable a part of the fanciful world of Mannerist gardens as elaborate iconographical programs and water-powered statuary. Although some were more erotic (or even obscene) than others, they were always calculated to catch visitors off guard, like those scurrying from water jets concealed on the terrace of the Fountain of Venus at Villa d'Este (above). Such contrivances demonstrated power over nature in an intriguing yet entertaining way.

Botanical gardens in Italy were laid out with the same feeling for elegance and proportion that permeates contemporary pleasure gardens. The one at Padua (left) today looks much as it did when Giovanni Moroni da Bergamo designed it in 1545 (opposite above). Surrounded by a wall, the central circular layout was subdivided into sixteen areas, each planted with a particular variety to help medical students with plant identification. By the 16th century, interest in the medicinal properties of plants had given way to botanical research as teaching gardens began to acclimatize exotic species. Padua's catalogue of 1591, the first ever printed in Europe, lists no fewer than 1168 plants, among them the dwarf fan palm that impressed Goethe during his travels in Italy.

schemes or flower color. Its mainstays were neatly clipped evergreens, such as yew and box, and enduring forms in stone and marble.

The Renaissance quest for knowledge about all forms of creation reawakened interest in botany and stimulated the appearance of gardens primarily devoted to rare and medicinal plants. Pisa led the way in 1543; Padua (1545) and Florence (1550) quickly followed suit. Although medicinal herbs were grown during the Middle Ages, particularly in monastic gardens, scientific classification was nonexistent and people relied on the "doctrine of signatures" in which a plant's medicinal use was indicated by its supposed resemblance to a specific human organ or part of the body.

Humanists cast their scholarly eye on nature and began to observe and investigate the morphology (or structure), geographic origins, and growth habits of plants. A number of knowledgeable amateurs made significant contributions to botanical research; one such study, now treasured by the Biblioteca Marciana, was compiled by a Venetian senator.

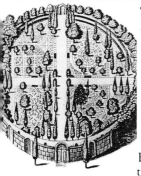

The Baroque: Art of an Expanding Universe

In the late 16th century, Galileo Galilei, Isaac Newton, and Johannes Kepler transformed world views and jolted religious beliefs. The demise of the finite universe brought humankind face to face with limitless space. The Baroque concept of movement through ever-expanding space had a decisive impact on architecture and, by extension, landscape design. It was to redefine the way Europeans looked at their natural surroundings.

A child of Rome, Baroque art emphasized spectacle over contemplation, illusion over reality. Lavish display was the keynote of the 17th century. Sprawling parks were laid out at Villa Borghese (begun 1605) and around Villa Doria-Pamphili (begun 1634). Contemporary town planning and church-building projects opened up dramatic outdoor spaces on a grand scale, a world of illusionistic effect in which gardens played a subordinate role. To find

Monsters stalk the eerie garden that an unknown architect and sculptor laid out for Vicino Orsini at Bomarzo about 1560 (below). The pagan Sacro Bosco, or sacred woods—a rocky slope strewn with colossal carvings of bizarre creatures, deities, and giants, some hewn out of solid rock—is as inscrutable now as it probably was then.

Baroque garden design, we must travel several miles south of the city, to Frascati.

The Villas of Frascati

In 1620 villas once again dotted the site of the old Etruscan town of Tusculum, as they had in the days of the Roman Republic. None more completely capture the spirit of the new era than Villa Aldobrandini.

At Villa Aldobrandini (begun 1598), the stylistic transition from Renaissance to Baroque dramatically unfolds as the visitor proceeds from one level to the next. The garden layout of Aldobrandini is focused on the house—a concept that would reappear in 17th-century France. The formality in front of the house, with its breathtaking view of the town and surrounding countryside, yields in back with Baroque drama to the famed semicircular "water theater" with fountains, elaborate water cascades and channels, and niches containing statues. The idea of a stage for water displays recalls the classical

"If you wish to see something superb, leave Rome and go to Tusculum, now Frascati," wrote J. T. Sprenger in 1660, betraying an enthusiasm shared by travelers from John Evelyn to Goethe. One of the marvels awaiting them was the Water Theater that is the central feature of Villa Aldobrandini's Baroque garden (above). A large semicircular retaining wall cut into the hillside behind the villa forms an amphitheater with five niches containing statues and water displays.

Sites of sacred rites in ancient Greece (Crete, Eleusis), grottoes evolved into artificial decorative elements in classical Rome and were therefore among Alberti's recommended garden features. A splendid 16th-century example is in Florence at the Boboli gardens. The Grotta Grande contains a series of three chambers showing the forces of nature; figures emerge dripping from the cave walls. Michelangelo's unfinished statues of slaves (now copies) stand in the first chamber, and Venus, interrupted in her bathing (below), is in the innermost chamber.

parallel drawn between theatrical design and garden design. Carved out of the steep wooded hillside, the theater merges into the Arcadian setting beyond. The melding of the tame garden and the wild woods beyond is an entirely Baroque touch.

Baroque Variations in Italy

In Florence, too, innovative garden design was alive and well. The Boboli Gardens and the wonderful Grotta Grande, a series of three "rooms" leading to a statue of Venus by Giovanni da Bologna, date from this period. Laid out in 1652, the monumental garden of Villa Garzoni, a Baroque gem in the Tuscan countryside near Lucca, features a dramatic rough-hewn water staircase; the clipped hedges and formal parterres eventually give way to wilderness at the top of the hill.

Salomon de Caus designed the Hortus Palatinus, Heidelberg (left), for Frederick V (ruled 1610–23) in 1615. The overall garden layout was supposed to represent the elector's possessions and included statues representing the Rhine, Neckar, and Main rivers which flowed through his territories. Through his gifted artisans, a ruler harnessed, reordered, and subordinated the natural landscape to his authority in the spirit of imperial Rome.

However, in the villas designed by Andrea Palladio, bordering the Brenta, near Venice, architecture and landscape were still governed by a unified design based on the Renaissance theory of beauty: The lines and proportions of the interior of the house are simply carried over into the space around it.

The Italian Garden Spreads Beyond Italy

By the 16th century, gardens in France, England, and the Netherlands shared many characteristics. Tunnel arbors, raised beds, square enclosures, and other medieval features were gradually giving way to the new Renaissance style as Italian artists emigrated to other European countries after the Italian Wars. Charles VIII of France and his army were deeply impressed by the villas and gardens they saw when they invaded the kingdom of Naples in 1495. The skilled gardeners and artisans who followed the king and his retreating army back to France later that year brought with them a fresh conceptual system that would underlie early French translations of the Italian garden vocabulary.

Salomon de Caus

Salomon de Caus, a French Hugenot, was a crucial link between Italy and the rest of Europe. He traveled in Italy before 1605, the year he entered the service of Archduke Albert in Brussels, and after 1610 went to

England. There he worked for the royal family (Henry, Prince of Wales, at Richmond Palace and Queen Anne at Somerset House and Greenwich Palace) and for Robert Cecil at Hatfield House. When James I's daughter, Elizabeth, married Frederick V, the Elector Palatine, in 1613, de Caus followed her to Heidelberg and there designed the phenomenal Hortus Palatinus, which sadly does not survive.

Isaac de Caus, probably a brother or nephew to Salomon, was thoroughly familiar with the plan of the garden (published 1620) by the time he, too, decided to go to England. Like the one at Heidelberg, Isaac's layout for the garden of Wilton in Wiltshire, another Late Renaissance masterpiece, bowed to a single imperative: an alignment that ensured a central point of view towards the garden. This was to be the cornerstone of the classic French garden, the glory of 17th-century Europe.

A manuscript by Johann Walther the Elder celebrates his patron Johann of Nassau's botanical collection and gardens at Idstein, near Frankfurt-am-Main (above, a Baroque grotto; below, a garden with beds in the shape of fruit and leaves). Idstein's fancifully laid out beds are filled with flowering plants, and here lies the chief difference between the architectural, evergreen parterres of Renaissance France and Italy and their counterparts in northern Europe.

The age of Louis XIV set garden design on the path of revolutionary change. The scale and magnificence of the settings that the king demanded as a backdrop for his court became the models for all of Europe. The formal gardens of 17th-century France transformed the natural landscape into a balanced, controlled work of art, a metaphor for humanity's dominion over nature.

CHAPTER IV

FORMALITY TRIUMPHANT: THE CLASSIC FRENCH GARDEN

The "hermitage" André Le Nôtre designed at Marly (opposite) as a retreat for Louis XIV proved more costly than Versailles. Karlsruhe (right), in Germany, was originally the hunting lodge of Margrave Carl Wilhelm of Baden-Durlach.

The Union of Garden Art and Architecture

Political and social conditions have unquestionably influenced the history of garden-making. Enclosed gardens and walled parks, for example, were a response to turbulent times. But we must also factor in a period's architectural style, because architects were often responsible for designing not just buildings but the space around them: Witness Leon Battista Alberti's work in 15th-century Florence, Giacomo Barozzi da Vignola's Villa Lante, and Pirro Ligorio's Villa d'Este, to name but a few. The notion that one person should be in charge of conceiving and executing a project's

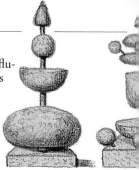

overall design stemmed from the Vitruvian theory of beauty as a harmonious relation of all parts to a coherent whole.

Alberti's pronouncements were considered as authoritative in France as they had been in Renaissance Italy. There, too, architecture had taken precedence over horticulture. The principle that the execution of a comprehensive design required a collaborative effort guided and orchestrated by the architect was established in France by Philibert de l'Orme while working for King Henry II's mistress, Diane de Poitiers, at the Chateau d'Anet (begun 1546). In the meantime, the king's wife, Catherine de Médicis, brought Italian influences to bear on French gardening practices.

At Versailles, rows of yew or small trees trimmed into a variety of shapes were planted on both sides of the parterre along the Tapis Vert ("green carpet" or lawn) leading down to the Bassin d'Apollon. At Marly, the art of topiary (above and below) as an architectural ordering of nature reached new heights of perfection. This technique of training and clipping evergreens into whimsical subjects (in Italy) or geometric figures (in France) can be traced directly to the gardening practices of Virgil's Rome. At the Luxembourg gardens in Paris, the initials of Marie de Médicis were spelled out in shaped box.

Garden Embroidery: The *Parterre de Broderie*

The key to the new French style of formal garden was the ornamental parterre, or garden bed, which was invariably fashioned from box and completely subordinated to a building's plan and siting. While the parterre had been an important element of the Renaissance garden, planted in geometric forms, the French took it to new heights, elaborately shaping plantings in what came to be called *broderie*, for its resemblance to

"embroidery." The style was also particularly well suited to the relatively flat expanses of the Loire valley and the environs of Paris. As extensions of architecture into the

The Medici family of Florence was instrumental in introducing Italian garden design to France. The Tuileries gardens (left) were created for Henry II's wife, Catherine de Médicis (the figure in black), who also made major improvements at Fontainebleau (opposite left). Salomon de Brosse began the Luxembourg palace and gardens for Henry IV's wife, Marie de Médicis, who was homesick for the Pitti Palace and its Boboli gardens in Florence.

surrounding space, parterres were best appreciated from the *piano nobile*, a building's upper-floor formal reception rooms. This was a departure from the thinking behind Italian gardens, which were designed primarily

to be viewed from garden level and emphasized vertical, rather than horizontal elements. In French gardens geometric compartments with squares, ovals, circles, and volutes were regimented into flawlessly symmetrical patterns that bowed to the needs of an overall plan.

The whimsy and lightheartedness of the "vegetable gardener" (below) and "flower seller" (opposite below) contrast with the pervasive geometry usually associated with formal gardens during the reign of Louis XIV. To the left is an engraving from Claude Mollet's book of garden plans.

THÉÂTRE
DES PLANS
ET IARDINAGES
CONTENANT
DES SECRETS ET DES INVENTIONS
incognuës à tous ceux qui jusqu'à present se sont meslez d'escrire sur cette matiere?
Auec vn Traicté d'Astrologie, propre pour toutes personnes, & particulierement pour ceux qui la culture des Iardins.

Nothing could be added or taken away. The colorful designs of English knot gardens and the verticality of Italianate gardens were banished and replaced throughout France by the classic balance and disciplined unity first described in Olivier de Serres's *Théâtre d'Agriculture* (1600).

The Emergence and Influence of Gardening Dynasties

Olivier de Serres's practical guide for laying out gardens included illustrations of parterres designed by royal gardener Claude Mollet. His father, Jacques Mollet, had made the first known *parterre de broderie* at Anet at the end of the 16th century after a design by Etienne du Pérac, architect to Diane de Poitiers' grandson, the duc d'Aumale. This earliest documented example of the symbiotic relationship between architect and head gardener—the first of many in garden history—is recounted in Claude Mollet's *Le Théâtre des Plans et Jardinages*, published posthumously in 1652. As he worked under his

father and du Pérac, young Claude assimilated the revolutionary concept that "an entire garden could not be other than a single compartment, divided up by the principal walks." Garden art stood at the threshold of genuine unity. Mollet's book, however, confined itself to practice and techniques; designing gardens still lay within the architect's sphere of authority. The outstanding figure of the following generation was Claude's son, the renowned André Mollet, who worked in England at St. James's Palace and Wimbledon House and in the Netherlands before Louis XIII (ruled 1610–43) appointed him *premier jardinier du roi* or first gardener to the king.

A number of Renaissance-inspired garden-design principles were embraced at the chateau of Conflans (above): water, decorative elements of stonework and sculpture, and an orderly grid of avenues and walks, all controlled by perspective.

A Name of Distinction: Le Nôtre

The other prominent family of royal gardeners, the Le Nôtres, were, like the Mollets, associated with Catherine de Médicis' newly laid out Paris garden of the Tuileries. Pierre Le Nôtre was put in charge of the parterres nearest the palace and much of the trellis work. His son and successor, Jean lived in a house adjoining the Tuileries and raised his children there. His daughters married other master gardeners.

Jean's son André, whose expertise, accomplishments, and fame earned him great prestige in his own lifetime, remains to this day the most famous figure in world gardening history. Interested in painting as a young man, André Le Nôtre entered the studio of Simon Vouet, where Charles Le Brun was a fellow student. Shortly after his appointment to his father's post at the Tuileries, he met architect François Mansart, who was so impressed by the young man's remarkable gifts that he secured a number of commissions on his behalf.

The Grandeur of an Ill-Fated Masterpiece

Le Nôtre's first great garden, Vaux-le-Vicomte, was a triumphant collaborative project with architect Louis Le Vau and painter Charles Le Brun. Nicolas Fouquet, Louis XIV's minister of finance and a man of extraordinary taste, brought together this accomplished trio to create for himself a country estate

L e Nôtre (below) conceived of Vaux (and later Versailles) as a setting for large outdoor garden fêtes, a vast theater in which royals and courtiers could make graceful entrances and exits.

on a scale unparalleled at the time. The completed building and grounds were proudly shown to King Louis (ruled 1643–1715) and his court on 17 August 1661 during a celebration as dazzling as Vaux itself.

Fouquet's unabashed display of extravagance was bound to have tragic consequences. The minister's vanity and megalomania aroused young Louis's jealousy and suspicion. Three weeks later, on 5 September, Fouquet was arrested for treason and spent the rest of his life in prison. Vaux-le-Vicomte came to symbolize an unforgivable affront to royal authority, but it was also a prelude to Versailles—crowning achievement of the classical age of France.

A Gardener, Not an Architect, Had the Say at Vaux

As he laid out the grounds of Vaux-le-Vicomte, Le Nôtre's guiding principle must have been unity. The building is scaled to fit in with an overall composition; it neither dominates nor overwhelms the surrounding area. It is Le Nôtre's garden, not Le Vau's chateau, that creates an illusion of unbounded space. From the house a central axis leads the eye toward a seemingly limitless vista

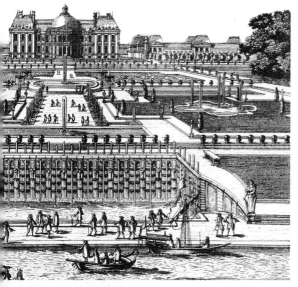

From the dome of the chateau, the main axis of the garden at Vaux bisects a *parterre de broderie* and continues toward a centrally located fountain before intersecting an ornamental canal running perpendicular to it. It then bisects a second, surprisingly plain parterre with matching oval water basins and leads to a large square basin. At this point, just before the ground slopes up, Le Nôtre placed a slender water channel, a wall, and low, wide steps descending to the Grand Canal, another major cross-axis that stretches into the distance. On the far side of the canal stands the Grotto with its fountains, and a third transverse axis is implied by a terrace, facing the Grandes Cascades. The symmetry of the central axis at Vaux is broken by secondary east–west axes at right angles to it. The first descended in three stages to a water garden once focused on a water basin and the Fontaine de la Couronne (opposite above). The second, a walk crossing below the *parterre de broderie*, led on the west to the kitchen garden and on the east to a stairway of fountains known as the Grilles d'Eau.

dominated by a colossal statue of Hercules. The majestic Grand Canal, a major cross axis, cannot be seen from the chateau; like the Grandes Cascades, it comes into view, dramatically, as one approaches it. One of the fountains spouts a dome of water that echoes the dome atop the chateau. Sunlight plays across shimmering expanses of still water that mirror the fitful skies overhead. Statues and fountains infuse the grandiose ensemble with a sense of heroic unity. This masterly balance of art and nature is, more than anything else, a visible expression of human dominion over the natural landscape, a distillation of 17th-century French rationalism.

Louis so loved his gardens at Versailles that he wrote a guide to them, *La Manière de Montrer les Jardins* (Manner of Seeing the Gardens), which maps out the route of the royal promenade. During this daily ritual, Louis conducted personal business while enjoying the grounds (above).

Versailles: Hymn to the Glory of Louis XIV

Is it any wonder that the young king, still reeling with jealousy over the magnificence of Vaux, felt compelled to transform his father's little hunting lodge at Versailles into a palace that would reflect his own magnificence? He would turn Versailles into the new capital of his kingdom, the seat of the French government and the royal court. The feat of transforming a site described by the memoirist Duc de Saint-Simon as "the saddest and most barren of places, with no view, no water, and no woods" into a model for the whole of Europe would in itself demonstrate Louis's absolute authority. Fouquet's successor as minister of finance, Jean-Baptiste Colbert, warned Louis that a project of this magnitude would be prohibitively expensive. The king could not be swayed. The same three

artisans who had worked for Fouquet were summoned to carry out this colossal undertaking. Louis went so far as to have countless pieces of sculpture and a thousand young orange trees moved from Vaux to Versailles.

Le Brun was in charge of the sculptural program at Versailles from 1665 to 1683, but Le Nôtre was responsible for its "grand design." He respected the existing topography when possible (as when he made use of a natural hundred-foot drop from the Palace to the Grand Canal to create a series of terraces), but elsewhere radically altered the natural landscape (as when he hollowed out a vast amphitheater for the Parterre de Latone). Plant material was relentlessly clipped into an architecture of outdoor walls (*palissades*), rooms (*cabinets de verdure*), and stately avenues, or *allées*. The king thought so highly of Le Nôtre that at the age of sixty-two, he climbed into his three-wheeled chair of state and personally escorted his eighty-eight-year-old gardener—whom he had granted the rare privilege of a sedan chair—on a final tour of the grounds.

The Sun King

The king had chosen the sun as his emblem, and it was to provide the iconographic program for Le Nôtre's

Le Nôtre laid out the main axes of Versailles to coincide with the points of the compass. The seemingly limitless vista from the windows of the Grande Galerie stretches toward the setting sun. To the south he opened a vista to the summer sun, across the terrace of the Orangerie (below) and on to the heights of Satory, where a monumental waterfall was to have been built.

The rigorously organized splendor of Versailles testifies not only to the genius of Le Nôtre, but to Louis XIV's determination to triumph over the natural landscape of the region around Paris. Every garden or park is a complex of signs, but they defy comprehension unless we know something about their social context, the owner's or patron's temperament and compulsions, and prevailing attitudes towards nature. Versailles mirrors a period in French history during which the monarchy wielded absolute power over political, social, and artistic life. The humiliation the young king had suffered during La Fronde—a series of uprisings aimed at limiting royal authority —made him wary of both the nobility and Paris. Louis was twenty-three when Fouquet flaunted Vaux, prompting the king to move the royal residence to the inhospitable site of Versailles. If, as the reproachful Saint-Simon once put it, the king "rode rough-shod over nature," his motive was to demonstrate dominion over his residence, his court, and, in a wider sense, his kingdom. Versailles, the memoirist observed elsewhere, was a "political device" calculated to keep courtiers amused— and muzzled.

design. The main axes of the overall layout correspond to the points of the compass; the limitless vista from the windows of the Grande Galerie extends towards the setting sun. Everything refers in some way to the sun god Apollo, from the ornamental elements within the tall hedge walls of the *cabinets de verdure* to the sculptural and architectural features throughout the park. His sister Diana, goddess of the hunt, served as a mythological allusion to the Bourbons' passion for hunting. This cult of Apollo lent itself to countless variations on the theme of the passage of time, including the hours of the day, the months and seasons of the year, and the seven ages of man.

Horticulture Survived Despite Architecture

Advances in hydraulic engineering further strengthened the 17th-century French garden ideology that the natural landscape should be an extension of architecture. In light of this overwhelming emphasis on enforced geometry, horticulture seems to have been relegated to a secondary role. However, for all the boxwood parterres, all the *allées* lined with wall-like hornbeam hedges, all the neatly clipped trees and shrubbery, formal gardens were by no means flowerless. In fact, no matter how far Le Nôtre's many projects took him from Paris, it was his contractual duty to keep the garden of the Tuileries filled with flowers year round.

Practicality and pleasure: the royal kitchen garden, designed by la Quintinie (above), and a party in the maze at the chateau of Chantilly, Le Nôtre's favorite garden (right).

Botanical and Kitchen Gardens Fit for a King

Louis was infatuated with all aspects of gardening, and Versailles would have been incomplete without an Edenesque allusion to nature's bounty. In 1670 he appointed lawyer, botanist, and author Jean-Baptiste de la Quintinie as *intendant pour les soins des jardins fruitiers*

et potagers (keeper of fruit and vegetable gardens) and set him the task of designing a royal kitchen garden.

The process of laying out, constructing, and planting the Potager du Roi lasted more than five years. Those cultivating the king's fruits and vegetables outside the palace were held to the same exacting standards imposed on craftsmen working within it.

A discriminating collector of plants and trees, Louis XIV

The linchpin in Le Nôtre's grandiose scheme for Versailles as the king envisioned it was a plentiful supply of water. After a series of disastrous projects, work began on the Machine de Marly (above), a gigantic hydraulic engine on the Seine. River water was lifted from this pumping station at Bougival to the aqueduct of Marly and from there channeled to Versailles' fourteen hundred fountains. Even then, there was never sufficient pressure for all of them to operate at once, so *fontainier* Claude Denis had standing orders to limit displays to those that came into the king's view as he toured the grounds.

substantially enlarged the Jardin du Roi (renamed, after the French Revolution, the Jardin des Plantes) that Gui de la Brosse, physician to Louis XIII, had established in Paris in 1626. He personally sponsored plant-collecting expeditions that had instructions to bring back botanical

The park of the Chinese emperor Yuan Ming Yuan was enlarged and embellished by Emperor Qian Long, a garden enthusiast. In 1747, enthralled by Father Giuseppe Castiglione's paintings of European gardens, he asked French and Italian Jesuits in Peking to design a scaled-down Versailles for his summer residence (detail, left above). There was a reciprocal fashion for chinoiserie pavilions in Europe. The short-lived Porcelain Trianon (left below) built in 1669 at Versailles was sheathed with blue and white tiles.

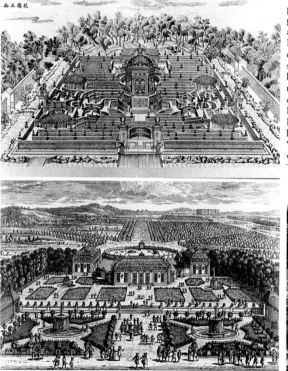

specimens from the New World and the Far East for acclimatization in Paris. Exotic plants from abroad would later inundate Europe.

The Influence of Versailles

Versailles was too sprawling, too complex, and its symbolism too heavy-handed, but the French formal garden had scored an overwhelming victory just the same. Rulers throughout Europe and even beyond were intent on possessing a Versailles of their own. The model they emulated, however, could hardly be duplicated. More often than not, these translations of Versailles were quite different in scale and adapted to local topography, regional traditions, and their patron's temperament.

The spirit of the Sun King's creation permeates Blenheim Palace (England), which Sir John Vanbrugh began in 1705 and "intended as a monument of the Queen's glory." During a trip to France, Peter the Great of Russia (ruled 1672–1725) succumbed to Le Nôtre's design while a guest at the Grand Trianon and appointed the Frenchman Jean-Baptiste Le Blond "architect general" of his new capital, St. Petersburg. Le Blond laid out the gardens and park for the royal summer palace, Peterhof, before his premature death three years later. This scaled-down Versailles features monumental fountains and cascades, while a long canal modeled on the Grand Canal unites the palace with the Baltic Sea beyond. Another Versailles-inspired garden, the delightful summer retreat of La Granja, near Madrid, was laid out as a water garden of canals and fountains for Louis XIV's grandson, Philip V of Spain (ruled 1700–46). The formal gardens at Caserta, near Naples, were designed for his son Charles III (ruled 1759–88). Le Nôtre's influence

The French formal garden took the whole of Europe by storm: from Russia, Peter the Great's "Versailles on the Baltic," Peterhof (below), to Austria (sprawling Schonbrunn, Vienna) and Germany. Frenchmen helped design the extensive gardens of Nymphenburg and Schleissheim, outside Munich, as well as Schwetzingen.

reached all the way to America: Pierre L'Enfant's design for Washington, D.C. is based on the *patte d'oie* (goose's foot)—a series of radiating avenues that was used often in the gardens of Le Nôtre.

Hans Vredeman de Vries' *Hortorum Viridariorumque…* (1583, left) is a garden pattern book, including cutwork parterres, designed to display tulips and other flowers. Tulips (engraving below left) became enormously popular early in the 17th century.

The Italian Legacy

Although occasionally blended with "formal" French elements or vernacular features, the Italian garden tradition continued to influence Germany and the Netherlands until the 18th century. Northern Europe, particularly England, remained under the sway of the Dutch, who had taken the lead in horticultural research. (A Dutchman, William of Orange, had become King William III of England in 1689.) The Netherlands had its version of the Renaissance garden —the scholar Erasmus described one in *The Godly Feast* (1522)—but Christian symbolism prevailed over ungodly paganism. Renaissance gardens were followed by the Mannerist gardens so copiously pictured in the 16th-century pattern books of Hans Vredeman de Vries and exemplified by the gardens he laid out for Emperor Rudolph II in Prague. His chief contribution to garden art was the cutwork parterre, a type of bed specifically intended for the display of the rare, exotic, flowering plants that were the passion of his fellow Dutch compatriots.

Charles de L'Ecluse

Flemish humanist, physician, and botanist Charles de L'Ecluse was the first scientific horticulturist and served as superintendent of the Leiden Botanic Garden (established 1587). The exotic Middle Eastern bulbs and tubers he cultivated—hyacinths,

irises, lilies, gladioli, sunflowers, and especially tulips—transformed northern European gardens. The Dutch were as adept at dealing in plants as they were at studying them. They exercised an international monopoly on onions, a virtual currency at the time, and uncharacteristically got caught up in the tulip craze, reaping fortunes overnight and losing them just as quickly when the market collapsed in 1634.

Daniel Marot designed the gardens of Het Loo in the Netherlands for William of Orange between 1686 and 1695, around the time the hunting lodge was remodeled into a royal palace. Thanks to a splendid restoration, visitors today can still appreciate this hybrid of Renaissance and Baroque influences that resulted in a composite of Dutch layout and French decorative features (left and below). The flower bed designs are in the Mannerist style pictured in the pattern books of Hans Vredeman de Vries.

During the 18th century, garden art returned to the Arcadian rusticity of ancient Greece, the countryside of Rome, and classical mythology, all filtered through the idealizing gaze of philosophy and painting. Intellectuals, poets, aristocrats, and politicians all across Europe became garden fanciers. But landscape gardening, the style that rediscovered nature through painting, originated in England.

CHAPTER V

PLANTING PICTURES: THE ENGLISH LANDSCAPE GARDEN

Both the "landscape garden" created at Caserta in Italy (opposite) for Marie Caroline of Austria, queen of Naples, and the rustic Hameau (right)—a group of fake farmhouses contrived at Versailles for her sister, Marie Antoinette—date from the 1780s. The more relaxed English style was as influential in the 18th century as French formality had been in the 17th.

Origins of the Landscape Garden

Early in the 18th century, a growing discontent with
French formality cleared the way for a fresh approach to
garden design. Theoretically, landscape gardening derived
from idyllic paintings of the Roman countryside by such

mid-17th-century painters as
Claude Lorrain, Gaspard
Dughet (brother-in-law to painter Nicolas Poussin), and the
more dramatic Salvator Rosa.

In practice, the real impetus
was to come from the English
love of country life. The shift
from deer hunting in forests to
fox hunting through mostly
open meadows and brushwood
stimulated new thinking among
wealthy English landowners, a
new way of conceptualizing the
countryside. Until William Kent turned from painting to
designing gardens, however, the landscape was regarded
more as a pleasant panorama than as a poetic concept
rooted in classical mythology and philosophy. The leading
proponents of the landscape gardening movement, which
first surfaced in literature, were the Earl of Shaftesbury,
the influential essayist and politician Joseph Addison, and
poet Alexander Pope, all of whom
inveighed against the artificiality of

"Consult the *Genius* of
the *Place*," advised
poet Alexander Pope,
"...that *Paints* as you
plant, and as you work,
Designs" (*An Epistle to
Lord Burlington*, 1731).
William Kent rejected the
formal garden layouts
exemplified by Hampton
Court Palace (below left),
which soon looked
"antiquated" compared
with the nascent
"picturesque" style (above
left, one of his drawings
for Pope's Garden
at Twickenham).

An artistic movement could not have revolutionized garden design in England had the time not been ripe for social change and economic growth. A series of parliamentary acts led to the enclosure of large tracts of common land, significantly increasing the acreage available for landscaped parks. At the same time, improvements in transportation made traveling easier and stimulated the remodeling of country estates. Progress and prosperity lay in the hands of landowners who belonged to the dominant Whig party and believed that agriculture was the keystone of English economic life. Landscape gardening looked to painting for inspiration, particularly the works of Claude Lorrain (left), but it also had close links with Italian theater design. Views stretching into the distance and radiating walks were modeled on illusionary scenery: Chiswick House outside London transferred to a garden setting the stage of Andrea Palladio's Olympic Theater in Vicenza. Garden design in 18th-century England owed as much to Vitruvius and the Italian Renaissance as it did to landscape painters.

the French formal garden. Stephen Switzer's handbook *The Gardener's Recreation*, first published in 1715 and reissued three years later as volume one of *Ichnographia Rustica*, stimulated interest, setting forth the theory of the new approach soon to be applied by William Kent and Lancelot ("Capability") Brown. Pioneering landscape designers Charles Bridgeman and Kent belonged to influential literary coteries. Another prominent figure, Horace Walpole, declared that "Poetry, Painting, and Gardening or the science of Landscape, will forever by men of Taste be deemed Three Sisters, or the *Three New Graces* who dress and adorn Nature."

A New Informality in England

The first to put these new ideas into practice, to reject both the prim symmetry of French classicism and old walled Renaissance gardens whether princely or private, was Charles Bridgeman. As royal gardener to George II (ruled 1727–60), he left existing layouts much as they were. But his thirty-odd designs for private clients, among them Blenheim, Claremont, and Rousham House, are infused with the innovative spirit of a new era. Walpole praised his "many detached thoughts that strongly indicate the dawn of modern taste," and hailed his use of the "ha-ha" as the "capital stroke, the leading step to all that has followed." Derived from the *saut de loup*, "jump of the wolf," a 17th-century French military invention, the "ha-ha," or dry ditch, was in effect a sunken fence that demarcated the boundaries of an estate without requiring a visible fence, thereby opening up uninterrupted vistas and literally clearing the way for greater freedom in landscape design.

Stowe: Monument to an Era

Stowe in Buckinghamshire is one of the outstanding landscape gardens of Europe. In the 18th century it was enlarged and transformed by four successive members of the Temple family, who drew on the expertise of the foremost practitioners of "picturesque" design. Better than any other, this park illustrates through its phases the evolution of landscape gardening, and the transition in taste, during this entire period. Richard Temple, 1st Viscount Cobham, inherited the estate in 1697. Soon after marrying a wealthy heiress, he began actively making improvements, combining an English squire's interest in the daily operations of his estate with a patron's receptiveness to

Lord Cobham (below, seated figure in right foreground) listens to Charles Bridgeman, landscape architect of his estate at Stowe, present the Rotunda. Over the course of the 18th century, the three giants of "picturesque" landscape gardening—Bridgeman, Kent, and "Capability" Brown—turned Stowe into the best-known, most-visited garden in England.

new ideas. His position as a
leading figure in the Whig
establishment imbued the design
concept of Stowe with symbolic
meaning, particularly its many garden
buildings: these temples for the Temples
are as much monuments to family pride
and wit as they are to a political
ideology. He then called on Bridgeman
and an old friend, Sir John Vanbrugh
(later active at Blenheim and Castle Howard)
to serve as garden designer and architect, respectively.
Together they took full advantage of the irregularities and
drawbacks of the site and created a masterpiece.

A corner of Bridgeman's plans for Stowe.

The Triumph of the "Picturesque"

William Kent, who began working at Stowe in 1735, started out as an apprentice painter and went on to study painting and architecture before turning his attention to garden design. While living for almost ten years in Italy he was greatly

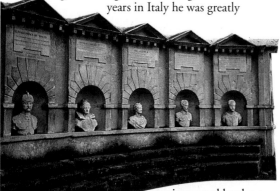

impressed by the theatrical quality of Italian gardens. Back in England, his proposed remodeling of the hillside at Chatsworth in Derbyshire—with a replica of the Sybil's temple at Tivoli above a cascade modeled on Villa Aldobrandini's water staircase—is an English translation of Italian garden vocabulary, transplanted to the English countryside.

The lessons Kent had learned in Italy led him to concur with his friend Pope's proclamation that "all gardening is landscape painting." Kent lacked both horticultural expertise and practical knowledge of garden layout; he could scarcely tell an oak from a willow. But his extraordinary eye more than made up for it. His painterly approach would free garden design not only from the last traces of English Renaissance formality but from the influence of the Dutch.

Even more eloquently than Stowe, the park Kent laid out in 1738 for General James Dormer at Rousham House, Oxfordshire, testifies to his gift for creating idealized picture settings. Here, as Addison had recommended, was "a whole estate thrown into a kind of garden," one which (to use Pope's expression) "called in" the surrounding countryside.

About 1735, architect William Kent transformed a little valley at Stowe into an "Elysian Fields" for his wealthy client. The allegorical garden buildings dotting the area, such as the Temple of Ancient Virtue and the Temple of British Worthies (left), make a political statement. Kent achieved a

newfound freedom by working "without level and line" (Sir Thomas Robinson, 1735).

The far more modest scale of Stourhead (below and the Pantheon, left) lent itself to a unified design concept. With

A Landowner Tries His Hand at Landscape Design

Lord Cobham and other Whig landowners were convinced that natural beauty could coexist with profitable agricultural management. The grounds of Castle Howard, North Yorkshire, which surpassed in scale even Blenheim and Stowe and afforded "the grandest scenes of rural magnificence" (Horace Walpole), were created by the 3rd Earl of Carlisle, an amateur attuned more to epic poetry than to the visual arts. His treatment of Wray Wood as a natural labyrinth and his meandering

no professional assistance, Henry Hoare I and II, who came from a prominent banking family, brought the idealized picturesque "scene" to a new level of perfection. Stourhead was both an 18th-century theme park with Virgilian overtones and a Claude Lorrain landscape painting come to life.

approach to Terrace Walk at Castle Howard were conceptual breakthroughs. The park's extraordinary architectural features, notably Vanbrugh's Temple of the Four Winds and Nicholas Hawksmoor's Mausoleum, serve as visual pauses within the landscape. "Nobody had told me," Walpole enthused in a letter to George Selwyn (12 August 1772), "that I should at one view see a palace, a town, a fortified city, temples on high places, woods worthy of being each a metropolis of the Druids, the noblest lawn on earth fenced by half the horizon, and a mausoleum that would tempt one to be buried alive."

"Capability" Brown: The Genius of the Place

Lancelot "Capability" Brown attracted the attention of Lord Cobham, whose gardens at Stowe were already the most famous in England, and went to work for him as head gardener in 1741. Although William Kent was still living and supplying architectural designs for Stowe—notably the Temple of Venus, the grotto, and the Palladian Bridge—Brown was put in charge of carrying them through.

Before long, the young gardener was working for a number of Lord Cobham's Whig friends. By the 1750s, he was regarded as the foremost landscape designer of his time, a reputation that was to last until this death, some thirty years later. The fact that this period coincided with the estate-building boom made Brown's imprint on the country's landscape that much more indelible. He turned down an invitation to work in Ireland on the grounds that he was not quite yet finished with England. It was an overstatement, but not by much.

The outspoken pragmatic Brown swept away all vestiges of English Renaissance gardens with no hint of remorse. Formal Elizabethan gardens like the one once at Longleat House (shown below in its transformed state) were, sadly, forever lost to future generations.

Brown's habit of assuring prospective clients that their grounds had "great capabilities" speaks for the designer's singular thought processes, his visual feel for a site, his innate sense of where best to thin out or plant or position particular features. Moreover, Brown's technique of removing walls and hedges, thereby merging the area immediately around the house with the distant landscape beyond, was perfectly attuned to the quasi-religious

Lancelot Brown (below) got the nickname Capability from his habit of referring to the "capabilities" of prospective clients' grounds. His genius rivaled that of André Le Nôtre a century earlier. J.M.W. Turner painted Petworth Park,

West Sussex (center), designed by Brown.

attitude towards Nature emerging in Europe at the time.

Capability Brown shared his countrymen's fascination with water in the landscape but condemned Kent's regimentation of this natural element as a "disgusting display of art." Few projects fired his enthusiasm more than creating "natural" lakes like those at Longleat House and Blenheim Palace. He also manipulated trees with consummate skill and was particularly adept at positioning small wooded clumps in the middle distance to produce a seemingly natural effect.

Repton and the Total Landscape

Although as influential in their country as their counterparts were in France, English gardeners did not establish "dynasties." In fact, Brown's spiritual successor, Humphry Repton, became the leading English landscape designer of his time in a very roundabout way. Neither

An unsuccessful businessman in dire financial straits, Repton purchased a small country estate and there learned about the practical aspects of land

Kent nor Brown published their theories, and few of their working drawings or notes survive. Repton's legacy, however, includes not only his so-called Red Books but four illustrated publications, one of which contains a list of Brown's architectural works.

Repton's strength was his comprehensive grasp of the "character" of a place, the celebrated *genius loci*. He was the first to take into account, not just the lay of the land, but the residence and personality of individual clients. Moreover, when the squirearchy that had been the mainstay of his practice was displaced by a new ruling class as a result of the Industrial and Agricultural revolutions, he accommodated his philosophy to the changing face of rural England.

The Arcadian Garden

An influential advocate of "picturesque" gardening, poet and theorist William Shenstone brilliantly outlined its principles and offered practical advice in an essay entitled

management, read up on landscape gardening, and pursued his interest in botany. He was on the verge of bankruptcy when, one sleepless night, he decided to take up landscape gardening in hopes of filling the void left by the death of Capability Brown. His quick success (above, Repton's business card) was due not only to his ability, but to his original technique of presenting proposals to individual clients in specially prepared books bound in red Moroccan leather. The so-called Red Books were to become Repton's trademark.

The delicate water-color drawings in Repton's Red Books had movable "slides" so that clients could compare their grounds before and after the proposed improvement (left).

The *jardin anglais* (or *anglo-chinois*) that appeared in France late in the 18th century bore little resemblance to the English gardens that inspired them. French variations on the "picturesque" style anticipated the coming revolution, romanticism, symbolism, and even surrealism (below, the *folie*, or "whimsical structure," in Parc Monceau, Paris).

"Unconnected Thoughts on Gardening" (published posthumously in 1764). His own small, but much visited and admired landscape garden, The Leasowes, was a faithful application of what he termed the "three aspects" of landscape gardening: the "sublime," the "beautiful," and the "melancholy or pensive." The prescribed route through the "naturalized" Arcadian setting of his *ferme ornée* (ornamental farm) was a circuit walk punctuated by statues, benches, Gothic ruins, and inscriptions calculated to prompt visitors to pause and appreciate the scenery. A heated debate ensued at the end of the

Painting influenced garden art in France, too. A specialist in "ruin pieces," painter Hubert Robert branched out into landscape design (left). With its orchestrated "scenes" and "picturesque" garden buildings, the huge park *à l'anglais* at Méréville is an exercise in control far closer to Le Nôtrean principles than those espoused by English landscape gardeners. Below left, the "ruined" Column House at Désert de Retz.

century between those who favored this picturesque style and the Brownian landscapists.

The Royal Botanic Garden and the Landscape Garden Abroad

Founded in 1759, the botanic gardens at Kew were worked on by all the great garden designers of the day: Bridgeman, Kent, Brown, and William Chambers, who set a fashion for exotic "follies" (whimsical garden structures like gazebos) that spread throughout England and the Continent.

French philosopher and writer Jean-Jacques Rousseau saw the unspoiled natural order as an antidote to the corrupting effects of society. Meanwhile, in Germany, philosophers Schiller and Goethe celebrated a Romantic

Vue Perspective de la Colonne.

movement that embraced the naturalizing tendency of English landscape design.

The Marquis de Girardin began laying out his estate at Ermenonville, near Paris, after traveling extensively. His new landscaped garden, to this day one of the loveliest in all of France, was modeled on The Leasowes, which had enthralled him when he was in England. Girardin's gardens, too, had a circuit walk and a scattering of monuments and inscriptions. Rousseau's tomb, designed by Hubert Robert, remains the garden's focal point, the ultimate memorial not just to a man but to a period during which tombs and cenotaphs were the most favored and appreciated of all garden ornaments.

West of Paris lies the smaller, but equally famous Désert de Retz, a park created by Baron de Monville beginning in 1774. The estate, with its dramatic garden of winding paths and startling buildings, is a most bizarre romantic confection. There was an entrance grotto guarded by larger-than-life satyrs bearing torches and the main house, made to look like the ruined base of a column. The most elaborate building in the Désert was the Maison Chinoise, which was inspired by the *jardin anglo-chinois*, or the Chinese garden by way of England. Serious American gardeners toured Europe for inspiration, which they found principally in the English landscape style. Thomas Jefferson, a passionate gardener wrote in 1806 that it was to England "without doubt we are to go for models in this art."

A man of his time, Girardin was as conversant with contemporary literature and philosophy as he was with the classics. His landscaped estate at Ermenonville abounds in abstract symbols. Dedicated to Montaigne—*qui omnia dixit*, "who has said everything"—the Temple of Modern Philosophy was made to look unfinished to remind visitors that philosophy is unending. There was a column in memory of Rousseau (seen below with the Girardin family), whom the Marquis admired and invited to live with him. The Shrine of Reverie and the Bocage were created in honor of the philosopher who spent the last six weeks of his life at Ermenonville and was buried there on the Isle of Poplars.

The Industrial Revolution deprived the picturesque landscape gardens of a once pastoral world and ushered in an era of stylistic diversity, an eclectic century awash with new plant varieties and technical advances. Social democratization turned a luxury into an affordable pleasure, modified at the end of the 20th century by a growing concern for ecology and the natural environment.

CHAPTER VI

FROM ECLECTICISM TO MODERNISM

The Crystal Palace, designed for the Great Exhibition of 1851 in London, was an outstanding example of a public promenade (opposite). Parc André-Citroën, in Paris (greenhouse, right), is a study in contemporary garden design.

The Flower Garden Makes a Comeback:
John Claudius Loudon and the Gardenesque Style

Signaling the transition between the landscape ideal of the 18th century and the more classic tastes of the 19th, Humphry Repton's designs exemplified and contributed to changing fashions. Increasingly self-confident but always mindful of his clients' needs, Repton changed his style in later years and even ventured to reinstate the fountain, symbol of the artificiality once shunned by the previous generation. Although his extended views were still based on those of Capability Brown, Repton reintroduced terraces, balustrades, and flower beds in the area adjacent to the residence; no longer did rolling lawns sweep up to the very walls of the manor house. "One may, with moderation, allow regular and artificial flower gardens," he declared in 1803.

The most influential designer after Repton's death in 1818 was John Claudius Loudon, an indefatigable man with an encyclopedic mind. He published approximately sixty million words on horticulture, garden history, architecture, and agriculture, most notably his

This view of Humphry Repton's cottage in 1816 (above) appeared as an "afterview" in one of his own celebrated Red Books. Flowers and colors had all but vanished from English garden design over the preceding two hundred years. Repton's quiet campaign to reintroduce color was to lead directly to the extravagant large-scale displays of the Victorian era.

Encyclopaedia of Gardening (1822), the first comprehensive treatment of the subject. In his youth Loudon advocated informal, irregular, picturesque designs. However, after traveling widely in Europe to study historic gardens, he acquired a taste for what he called "geometrical" layouts in the "ancient style," and their influence hastened the revival of formality in garden design. Loudon championed what he dubbed the "gardenesque" style in the popular *Gardener's Magazine*, which he founded in 1826. Based on the notion that each individual plant should be displayed to best advantage, this gardening—to be more precise, planting— philosophy encouraged orderly diversity. The moralizing tone of Loudon's periodical was typical of the prevailing Victorian ethic of edification and "improvement."

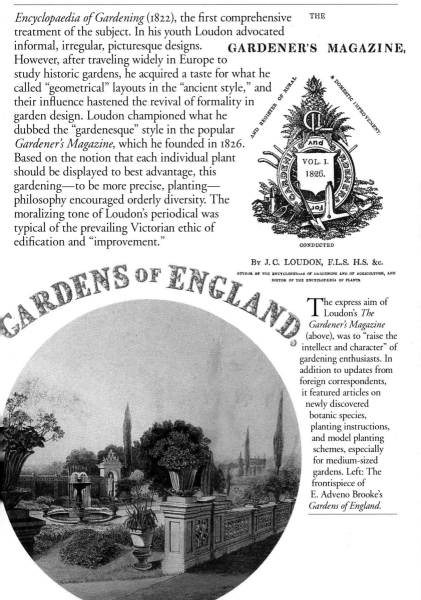

THE

GARDENER'S MAGAZINE,

AND REGISTER OF RURAL & DOMESTIC IMPROVEMENT.

VOL. I.
1826.

CONDUCTED

BY J. C. LOUDON, F.L.S. H.S. &c.

AUTHOR OF THE ENCYCLOPÆDIAS OF GARDENING AND OF AGRICULTURE, AND EDITOR OF THE ENCYCLOPÆDIA OF PLANTS.

GARDENS OF ENGLAND.

The express aim of Loudon's *The Gardener's Magazine* (above), was to "raise the intellect and character" of gardening enthusiasts. In addition to updates from foreign correspondents, it featured articles on newly discovered botanic species, planting instructions, and model planting schemes, especially for medium-sized gardens. Left: The frontispiece of E. Adveno Brooke's *Gardens of England.*

Excess and Exoticism: The Victorian Age

These illustrations from E. Adveno Brooke's *Gardens of England* (1856–7) testify to the decorative opulence of Victorian gardens. Garden architects made a dash for relics and ornaments from the Italian Renaissance and other bygone eras, but historical revivalism all too readily degenerated into pastiche and indiscriminate eclecticism. The imported exotic plants that started pouring into England about 1840 found ready use in the system of "change bedding"— elaborate, formal floral displays planted for temporary seasonal effects. The following gardens featured in Brooke's book are, opposite above: Eaton Park, Berkshire; below: Shrubland Park, Suffolk; above left: Wilton House, Wiltshire; overleaf above: Alton Towers, Staffordshire; overleaf below: Elvaston Castle, Derbyshire; and overleaf opposite: Trentham Hall, Staffordshire. The 4th Earl of Harrington's garden at Elvaston Castle boasted an arboretum with thousands of conifer species and a remarkable topiary collection surrounded by immense yew walls.

Mail-Order Gardens and New Exotics

The return of flower beds mid-century fostered both extravagance and exoticism. Mail-order firms offered a wide assortment of bedding patterns for "ready-to-plant" garden kits that included both appropriate plants and instructions for planting them. The unprecedented abundance of new varieties added welcome horticultural variety but, as one might imagine, tended to play havoc with form and color in gardens that reflected the Victorian passion for the ornate. England was inundated with imported plants. By the late 18th century, amateur

plant collectors had been largely replaced by trained botanists with detailed instructions to comb specific destinations for new varieties. A host of missionaries and explorers swelled their ranks. Commercial nurseries, which were expanding by leaps and bounds, dispatched plant hunters to every corner of the globe. The Royal Botanic Gardens at Kew, greatly expanded since its inception in 1759, and the Royal Horticultural Society (founded 1804) also sponsored plant-collecting expeditions.

Seed merchants were already doing a brisk mail-order business (left) when E. E. Budding patented his revolutionary lawn mower in 1830 (below). Both were essential factors in the democratization of gardening. Now everyone could have an impeccably groomed lawn.

New Inventions, New Trends

With the abolition of the Glass Tax in 1845, the greenhouse became an affordable—and, in the eyes of the English middle class, essential—adjunct to the home. The landed gentry also took to building these latter-day orangeries, not only for the pleasure of growing flowers for indoor display, but to acclimatize tender exotics and propagate a ready stock for "bedding out"—the practice of moving plants from green-

houses to outdoor beds in the warmer months. With the invention of the Wardian case (a sealed glass container), ninety percent of imported plants survived the journey to England. Small gardens proliferated, encouraged by the invention of the lawn mower in 1830 and the growing popularity of magazines put out by the burgeoning horticultural press. Although large-scale gardens were still in evidence, the average English citizen began to exhibit a devotion to, and proficiency in, small-scale gardening unmatched anywhere else but Holland. Gardening became the favorite pastime of an entire nation.

Gardening in France and the *Jardin Anglais*

Their estates in need of restoration, émigrés returning to Napoleonic France—a good many from England—opted for landscape gardening as a fashionable, less costly alternative to the formality of the past. But the

The "gardenesque" approach as Loudon initially proposed it— using exotics brought back to Europe in Wardian cases (below)— lent itself to incoherent, if not chaotic arrangements of trees, shrubs, and flowers (above, Battlesden Gardens).

Marie-Josèphe Rose Tascher de la Pagerie was born in Martinique and married Napoleon Bonaparte in 1796. In 1799 she acquired Malmaison, an estate at Bougival, near Paris. The future empress was a friend of botanist André Thouin, whose brother Gabriel codified the *jardin anglais* in France. Napoleon strongly objected to Joséphine's taste for landscape gardens, but she declared that if the Scottish gardener Thomas Blaikie could lay out the pre-Revolutionary Bagatelle for the Comte d'Artois, then she, too, was entitled to a fashionable garden *à l'anglaise*. Her contemporaries report that she was genuinely interested in botany, and her position gave her the wherewithal to collect plants from all over the world. She drew on the expertise of eminent botanists and the naturalist-explorer Aimé Bonpland, who had traveled with Alexander von Humboldt to South America and supervised her gardens at Malmaison and Navarre from 1806 to 1814. The 250 varieties of roses cultivated at Malmaison were immortalized by the renowned Belgian artist Pierre-Joseph Redouté. Left: Auguste Garneray's watercolors of the garden and conservatory.

real impetus came from Gabriel Thouin, whose system-atized *jardin anglais* linked a coordinated network of paths to a large circular walk around a lawn punctuated by clumps of vegetation. In the 1860s these island beds, which can still be seen in some French public parks, were adopted to imitate the English practice of carpet bedding—massed bedding of dwarf or creeping foliage for temporary seasonal effects. But French gardeners did not distinguish between carpet and flower bedding, and the result was a new composite style known as *mosaïculture.* The patterns were purely geometric at first, but a number of experimental displays at the World's Fair of 1878 set a fashion for zoomorphic and emblematic shapes. In Italy, biblical scenes executed in carpet bedding added extravagance to eclecticism.

Pleasure Gardens for the Masses: The Public Park Comes into Its Own

Of all the new trends spawned by this revival-minded century, few were as momentous as the philosophy that open spaces should be made available to the general public instead of the privileged few. Public promenades were not unknown in earlier periods of French history and by the 18th century were routinely included in town-planning projects, such as La Pépinière in Nancy. After the Revolution, parks formerly belonging to the aristocracy, the Crown, and the Church were

Variously patterned flower beds (above right) evolved into elaborate carpet-bedding designs. Prince Pückler's highly decorative "pleasure ground" at Muskau, bordering Germany and Poland, boasted outstanding examples of what German gardeners called *Teppichgartnerei*— or carpet gardens (above left).

remodeled into public promenades.

Emperor Joseph II opened the Prater in Vienna to the public in 1777: "A pleasure garden for all people, dedicated by your friend," proclaimed the inscription at its entrance. The rationale of the *Volksgarten* (People's Garden), as formulated by the Dane C. C. L. Hirschfeld, was to combine enjoyment of nature with visual glorification of a nation. This concept spread to Germany, where Peter Josef Lenné included in his 1819 plan for Berlin's Tiergarten a series of People's Halls with patriotic statues and war memorials.

The French pioneered the modern cemetery early in the 19th century, although its emergence actually dates from 1789, the year the city of Paris banned churchyard burial. The famous and widely imitated cemetery of Père-Lachaise opened in Paris in 1804. Such

Systematized by Gabriel Thouin, the functional *jardin anglais* (below, his proposal for enlarging the Jardin des Plantes in Paris) was to spread throughout France during the 19th century.

nondenominational burial parks were laid out informally with winding paths, groves of trees, carefully planned views, and an occasional pond or lake. Funerary inscriptions and monuments already dotted landscaped parks in the 18th century; now, of course, ornamental garden buildings were replaced by tombs. Cemeteries became gardens for both the dead and the living.

The English Public Park: Instrument of Social Reform

The first noteworthy advocate of public parks in England was John Loudon. "Till lately," he wrote in 1822, "Hyde Park was the only equestrian garden in Britain," not even a "well arranged" one at that. The pleasure gardens of the 18th century were open only to those who could afford to pay a fee. Royal parks, albeit theoretically open to the public, provided no seats or shelters. Loudon was instrumental in rallying support for the municipal park as an instrument of social reform. His Terrace Garden at Gravesend (1835) was the first publicly owned space in England used for promenades and a public botanical collection.

Emperor Joseph II opened Vienna's Prater (below) to the public in 1766 as "a pleasure garden [*Belustigungsort*] for all people, dedicated by your friend."

The first major public parks were laid out by Joseph Paxton, of Crystal Palace fame, who rose from humble beginnings to become at twenty-three head gardener to the 6th Duke of Devonshire at Chatsworth. There he experimented with revolutionary glasshouse design principles that architects were not to fully grasp, much less apply, until the 20th century. His first commission for a public park (Prince's Park, Liverpool) featured a new type of circulation system that carefully separated pleasure traffic within the park from city traffic. Paxton's best-known public park, Birkenhead Park (begun 1844), was the first publicly funded venture of its kind.

The Public Parks of Baron Haussmann

The first large-scale program aimed at integrating public parks into a city plan was implemented in France in the 1850s: Napoleon III's initiative to modernize Paris. As prefect of the Seine, Baron Georges-Eugène Haussmann created new tree-lined avenues, the sewer system, public promenades and parks, and forty-odd little public gardens scattered throughout the city.

In 1852 Napoleon III (ruled 1852–71) gave the Bois de Boulogne, which had been a royal forest until the

Joseph Paxton formed a company to enlarge the Crystal Palace to twice its former size and re-erect it as the centerpiece of a sprawling leisure park at Sydenham (above), which he hoped would draw millions of paying visitors. Its inordinate scale and spectacular attractions aspired to Versailles-like grandeur. Life-size concrete dinosaurs stalked an island in one of its two lakes, and members of the Royal Society once banqueted at a table set up in the belly of a reconstructed iguanodon. The park at Sydenham was the forerunner of 20th-century theme parks, such as Disneyland and its clones.

The city of Paris has Baron Haussmann's right-hand man, Jean-Charles-Adolphe Alphand (below), to thank for the beautiful public parks at Montsouris (left, painted by L. Vallée, 1900) and Buttes-Chaumont (opposite above). More an engineer than an artist, Alphand left his imprint on the urban landscape with the help of chief gardener Jean-Pierre Barillet-Deschamps, whose style of "decorative horticulture" made heavy use of large-leafed subtropical plants.

Revolution, to the city of Paris to be developed as an outdoor recreation area. Working under Haussmann, engineer and landscape architect Jean-Charles-Adolphe Alphand completely remodeled the two-thousand-acre Bois; Jean-Pierre Barillet-Deschamps advised him on planting and design. Together they profoundly altered the urban geography of the French capital. The system of concentric boulevards, the redesigned Champs-Elysées, the Bois de Vincennes and Parc Monceau, the gardens of the Champ-de-Mars, and the transformation of Buttes-Chaumont and Montsouris into parks are but a few of their achievements.

By the late 1860s, there was hardly a major city

in France and England that did not boast a public park. The rest of Europe and some colonies followed their lead stylistically, seldom straying from a derivative hybrid of 18th-century landscape park design and the beddings for subtropical varieties developed in private gardens back in the 1840s.

In 1858 Frederick Law Olmsted designed the first American public park, Central Park in New York City. His work was heavily influenced by that of Paxton's Birkenhead Park in Liverpool. Although the influence of these European public parks on future garden trends

Transformed from abandoned quarries, Buttes-Chaumont (below) was one of the parks Alphand described in *Les Promenades de Paris* (1867–73) and *L'Art des Jardins* (1886), in which he expounded his highly influential theories of landscape design. His path system was calculated to ensure

proved minimal, they left their imprint on the history of both cities and gardens and survive the world over as living testaments to 19th-century design solutions.

William Robinson Proposes the Wild Garden

The excess and extravagance of the Victorian period, with its regimented carpet-bedding schemes and overcharged eclecticism, sparked a strong reaction spearheaded by the

an orderly "continuous movement" from entrance to exit by way of points of view where "the line of vision is always at a tangent to the curve of the path." Alphand's repertory of subtropical plants included elephant's ear, *Colocasia bataviensis* (left).

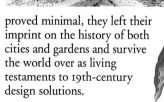

Napoleon III knew full well that the oases of greenery he inserted in the restless city of Paris were much more than pleasure grounds; they were part of a political agenda. Public parks held out the prospect of social harmony, or the illusion of it. The aesthetic rationale of modern city parks harks back to the timeless theme of the Garden of Eden: in this brilliant variation, it was hoped that relaxation and diversion in a natural setting would act as a safety valve for the tensions of urban life and perhaps neutralize its harmful effects. Thus, to the extent that municipal parks were calculated to socialize the masses and therefore keep them under control, the "Haussmannization" of Paris was part of a counter-revolutionary game plan. They were to prove enduringly popular just the same, and a city already acclaimed a great world capital grew even more beautiful. "Paris has become an Arcadia," rhapsodized an English tourist in 1869. Left: Jean Béraud's painting (c. 1900) of the Chalet du Cycle in the Bois de Boulogne.

Robinson's magnum opus, *The English Flower Garden*, was first published in 1883, ran to fifteen editions in his lifetime, and is still available today. It encouraged individuality in garden design

indefatigable William Robinson, a hot-tempered Irishman. Robinson combined the classic Victorian ethic of energetic diligence and reforming zeal with a forward-looking aversion to straitlaced garden design. By the 1860s the world of the Industrial Revolution was awash with mass-produced mediocrity. Robinson lamented that nature, once considered so threatening, was now itself jeopardized by contemporary taste.

by emphasizing interactions among plants and advised taking into consideration everything from a plant's size and shape to the color of its foliage and flowers. Tastefulness now worked in tandem with ecological concerns.

Permanent Planting

In *Alpine Flowers for Gardens* (1870), Robinson proposed planting alpine species in small rock gardens. They quickly became a much favored, if incongruous, addition to many an English garden. That same year, in *The Wild Garden*, he declared that a garden should not slavishly conform to a layout but instead encourage natural development and respect for plant color, form, foliage, and growing habits.

The Robinsonian philosophy of placing "perfectly hardy exotic plants under conditions where they will thrive without further care" was to play a fundamental

Like many others, Robinson was influenced by the Arts and Crafts movement led by John Ruskin and William Morris. A reaction to poorly designed, mass-produced objects, it sought to break down the distinction between art and craft and revitalize traditional English handicrafts. Its effects were felt in gardening as a renewed appreciation of vernacular cottage gardens and a shift from exotics to old-fashioned flowers. Although historically overshadowed by the Arts and Crafts movement, the vigorous collateral current of Edwardian neo-classicism left its imprint on many an English, Continental, and American garden during the 20th century. While "progressive" academics, artists, politicians, and amateurs contentedly endorsed smaller, simpler houses and naturalistic gardens, aristocrats and the rising class of well-heeled businessmen and industrialists clamored for grandiose displays that had to be culturally and historically "correct."

role in modern gardening. His insistence on informality (native and exotic plants mixed in the same bed, massed bulbs naturalized in grass), his subtle use of color, and most importantly, his concept of permanent planting as an alternative to the bedding system marked the beginning of the garden as we know it today.

The English Flower Garden

Robinson's philosophy reached a wider audience with the establishment in 1871 of his weekly journal *The Garden*. His naturalistic approach to garden design—using trees, rocks, water, and meadows—coupled with the growing availability of new plants, was to set a fashion for large

horticultural gardens by the turn of the century.

Robinson wanted to leave garden-making "to each gardener's individual imagination and ability to create his own private, personal wilderness." Considerations of taste now went hand in hand with ecological concerns. Relationships between plants were closely studied, large and small varieties knowledgeably juxtaposed. Plant form, foliage, and color were assessed as never before, resulting in a subtle sophistication that dissociated itself from picturesque garden practices and anticipated our belated interest in ecology.

The Battle Lines Are Drawn: "Natural" vs. "Formal"

Landscape architect Henry Ernest Milner published *The Art and Practice of Landscape Gardening* seven years after the first edition of Robinson's landmark *The English*

In 1883 Impressionist painter Claude Monet moved to Giverny in Normandy. With a painter's eye and a gardener's hands, he created a garden in the spirit of the informal cottage gardens which the Arts and Crafts movement had brought back into favor. The Clos Normand is a tangle of plants and colors, while the water garden mirrors the sky overhead.

Flower Garden. Contending that architects trammeled nature and that only a "landscape architect" could set it free, he advocated renewed appreciation of the beauty of the English countryside, just as Robinson had defended the use of native English flowers. This twofold attack was more than architects could bear. In January 1892 Sir

Reginald Blomfield published *The Formal Garden in England*, instantly establishing him as the champion of formality in gardening—and Robinson's archenemy. The landscape architect's objective, Blomfield argued, was not "to show things as they are, but as they are not." "It is evident," he wrote, "that to plant a garden the knowledge necessary is that of design, not of the best method of growing a giant gooseberry." The fierce controversy between the proponents of formality and a more natural approach has subtly shaped garden philosophy and practice to this day.

The Warring Factions Are Reconciled: The Gertrude Jekyll–Edwin Lutyens Partnership

Gertrude Jekyll was the most influential garden designer in England before World War II. A friend of Robinson's in the 1880s, she first met Edwin Lutyens, a young architect and landscape designer, in 1889. They became friends and collaborators. Motivated by her close working relationship with an architect, she concentrated her considerable talent on rethinking the naturalistic approach within a more formal framework. This was a

Endorsed by the famous critic and essayist Walter Pater in his *Studies in the History of the Renaissance* (1873), the classic Italian garden resurfaced as a viable design option. The "neo-Italianate" style spread to the United States, France, and the Riviera before returning to the land that inspired it: A splendid Renaissance-inspired garden was created for the pope's country residence at Castelgandolfo. The classical revival of the late 19th century was also a celebration of national identity and pride. French landscape architects Henri Duchène and his son Achille pioneered the restoration of French gardens in the classic style of the 17th century. Together they restored Vaux-le-Vicomte and helped reconstruct, among others, the parks of Courances, Le Marais, and Maintenon; Achille designed formal water-terraces for Blenheim. The two mainstreams at the time—formal design and informal planting—were to converge in the 20th century (left, Culpeper Garden, Leeds Castle, Kent, planned and planted by Russell Page).

South Front looking to Summer House

"When I was young," Gertrude Jekyll recalled, "I was hoping to be a painter, but to my lifelong regret, I was obliged to abandon all hope of this...on account of extreme and always progressive myopia." Her friendship and working partnership with young architect Edwin Lutyens was to be her consolation. When he designed her house, Munstead Wood, Surrey (left), the seasonally themed garden around it was well under way. Jekyll mixed and "under-planted" rose bushes, and knowledgeably and lovingly selected plants for her colorful herbaceous borders (opposite below, behind the Lutyens sketch of her, a planting scheme with irises and lupins for Munstead Wood). A profound gardening

philosophy shapes her exquisitely sophisticated exercises in informal planting, set within Lutyens's geometric framework.

major turning point in garden history. Although true to Robinsonian precepts (such as her continued use of native trees to maintain contact between the garden and the larger landscape beyond), her calculated informality was kept in line by the strict geometry of Lutyens's designs.

Thanks to Gertrude Jekyll, the herbaceous border, planted as close-set drifts of color and set against walls, earned popularity in the great gardens of late Victorian and Edwardian England. Influenced by the theories of the French chemist and director of the Gobelins tapestry works, Michel Chevreul, who devised color wheels to establish complementary colors and formulated the system of simultaneous contrasts, she developed single-color borders as well as planting schemes based on graded sequences of warm and cold colors. A Lutyens house with a Jekyll garden remains a symbol of the period.

Two Landmarks in Garden Design: Hidcote Manor and Sissinghurst

Major Lawrence Johnston, an American-born Briton, developed Hidcote Manor Garden on twelve hectares of farmland in the Cotswolds during the first half of the

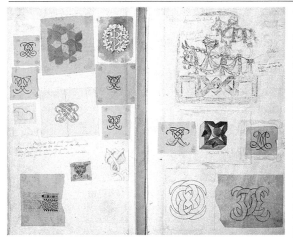

The Jekyll–Lutyens partnership (the younger Lutyens affectionately referred to Jekyll as "Aunt Bumps, Mother of All Bulbs") produced superb examples of English garden style that satisfied both the formalists and the more plant-oriented gardeners. Lutyens created a strong architectural "backbone" that disciplined Jekyll's spreading informal drifts without detracting from their central role in the overall composition. In her extensive sketchbooks (left) and writings—from her first book, *Wood and Garden* (1899), to her articles for *Country Life* and, finally, *Colour in the Flower Garden* (1908)—Jekyll set forth the theories that guided her experiments with form and color. Her work is

20th century. Aside from his wealth, all Johnston had to work with were an ancient Lebanon cedar, a few beech trees—and a great gift for garden design.

He also had the good fortune to count among his friends the intuitive, talented Norah Lindsay, an innovative gardener and garden designer. Together they resourcefully turned Hidcote's uncompromising T-shaped framework into a series of intimate outdoor rooms enclosed by luxuriant walls of greenery. Venturing beyond the safety of Gertrude Jekyll's carefully graded sequences of color and uniform textures, they planted informally against an impeccable, tapestry-like background of lawns and hedges. The result was

as relevant as ever and continues to inspire garden enthusiasts everywhere.

what Vita Sackville-West once called a "a jungle of beauty…controlled by a single mind."

The aristocratic writer Victoria (Vita) Sackville-West and her husband, writer and diplomat Harold Nicolson, bought a ruined Elizabethan manor house called Sissinghurst Castle in 1930 and set about creating a garden that would be an emblem of their love and refinement. It took years to clear out the rubble of the previous few centuries. Now acclaimed as the epitome of the modern British gardening tradition, this small garden attracts increasingly large numbers of visitors from all over the world. Its subtly colored, informal plantings are decidedly un-Victorian in character. The flower beds are set within a tightly controlled

M ajor Lawrence Johnston developed the plan of Hidcote Manor with Norah Lindsay. The garden consists of a series of small compartments scaled to the stone manor house; they are at once connected and separated by long axial grass walks (below) and lawns. Utter disorder might have resulted had the luxuriant plantings not been set within a tightly controlled framework of successive spaces and

architecture of outdoor "rooms" reminiscent of Hidcote; but the two gardens are worlds apart in spirit. Johnston's is an intellectual garden; Sissinghurst, a visible expression of its owners' personalities. Sackville-West's interests ranged far beyond her 17th-century ancestral home Knole in Kent. She had a passion for Renaissance Florence and traveled to Persia, where to her delight both magical paradise gardens and the rocky wilderness blazed with colorful wildflowers.

The architectural severity of the garden's overall design

ascending levels. Hidcote epitomized the heady period between the wars, when one could still while away the time in a paradise garden of one's own making.

came from Nicolson, whose eye for firm classical lines gave his wife the framework she needed. Restored after World War II, the gardens were opened to the public and a steady stream of somewhat awed visitors began. In 1946 Sackville-West began writing a column in the London newspaper *The Observer*. She wrote primarily about gardening, describing in great detail the progress of her beloved Sissinghurst, which was also a functioning farm. She continued writing the column for fourteen years. Sissinghurst is a symbol of order and beauty, a haven of peace and civilization.

Nicolson and Sackville-West wanted their garden to have not only a formal structure with extended views but a sense of privacy and intimacy. So they subdivided it into separate enclosures— such as the Rose Garden, White Garden (below, with the Tudor castle tower in the background), Orchard, Cottage Garden, and Nuttery— and planted each of them in the romantic profusion so dear to Sackville-West.

"We live under an accumulation of periods and styles and cultures." Russell Page contributed to all the major gardening trends of his century: renovation, adaptation, smaller private gardens, public projects, landscaped corporate parks, sculpture gardens. At the landscaped estate and sculpture garden he created for PepsiCo's world headquarters in Purchase, New York (water-lily garden, left), he not only designed the landscape and laid out the grounds but had a say in commissioning and selecting the sculptures. He sited individual pieces as if he were planting trees and positioned trees as if they were sculpture. After World War II, Page realized that industrialists and cities had taken over the role of patronage once played by popes and princes, that interest in gardening would become virtually universal, and that the space along highways or around service-station pumps should be as carefully thought out as large-scale gardens created for museums or wealthy individuals. An authentic garden-maker on an ever-shrinking planet, Page combined an innate sense of elegance and wide-ranging erudition with a flair for innovation and flashes of intuition.

The Last Great Garden-Maker of Our Century

The Englishman Russell Page, who died in 1985, was the foremost landscape architect of his time. Yet most people are not familiar with either his achievements or his eloquent book, *The Education of a Gardener* (1962). A rare combination of artist and expert horticulturist, Page is in a class by himself not only because his projects were so diverse but because of his command of European gardening traditions, his grasp of the Islamic garden, and his knowledgeable handling of trees and plants. He continually enriched our physical and cultural landscape.

Sculpture and the Modern Garden

Sculpture has always been welcome in the garden, but the 20th century witnessed a new phenomenon arising from the need to display sculpture to the public. To this end a number of private collectors established foundations (for example, Kröller-Müller Sculpture Garden in the Otterlo Forest, Netherlands). Another open-air museum, the Louisiana Museum in Denmark (named for the owner's three wives, all called Louise), deftly integrates unobtrusive architecture, mature trees, and sculptures into the landscape setting. Museums commissioned architects to create outdoor spaces for their sculpture (Philip Johnson at the Museum of Modern Art in New York, Isamu Noguchi at the Israel Museum in Jerusalem). Temporary public exhibitions of contemporary art in Oslo and Stockholm were developed into permanent sculpture parks.

Scottish poet, sculptor, and gardener Ian Hamilton Finlay (born 1925) has turned garden-making into an outlet for his many artistic gifts. His compositions include the "sacred grove" in the sculpture garden of the Kröller-Müller Museum in the Netherlands and the cubist garden at the Max Planck Institute in Stuttgart. His most comprehensive work is Little Sparta, his own continually evolving garden in the rugged Scottish countryside. To call it a sculpture garden, like the one Henry Moore designed for himself in Hertfordshire (left), would not do it justice, for it is meant to be appreciated as a total experience engaging the mind, the eyes, and the senses (above and on page 128).

A latter-day Arcadia has risen on a site formerly occupied by the Citroën automobile factory. In 1971, the city of Paris bought back the fifty-five acre parcel in the 15th arrondissement and immediately proposed creating a new district focused on a huge thirty-five acre park overlooking the Seine, a "partial reclamation of the green space of what used to be the Plain of Grenelle." An international search for professional designers ended in a tie between the team of Gilles Clément and architect Patrick Berger and that of Alain Provost, J.-P. Viguier, and J.-F. Jodry. Gilles Clément, the most theory-oriented of the new generation of French landscape architects, explained the park's conceptual framework and defined its four main "implementary criteria" as Nature, Movement (or Metamorphosis), Architecture, and Artifice. A concerted effort combining "the work of architects and the work of landscape designers" resulted in a logical progression of spaces governed by their relative proximity to the river (Nature) or the city (Artifice). A number of smaller theme gardens branch off from the rectangular lawn that forms the green core of Parc André-Citroën.

Urban Landscape Design: Beyond the Garden City

For centuries humankind has sought solutions to problems arising from the growth of cities. The ever-prescient Leonardo da Vinci, who studied Milan back in the 15th century, not only recommended satellite cities with no more than five thousand houses and twenty-five thousand inhabitants but proposed separating pedestrian from horse-drawn traffic.

These very ideas have since been implemented to help curb the growth of urban centers and relieve overcrowding. But another solution may hold the key. Baron Haussmann was the first in Europe to create parks as an integral part of a comprehensive plan for Paris, and the French capital has once again turned to this concept as a means of easing congestion. Work has begun on a large-scale urban renewal program that includes Parc de la Villette to the north and Parc André-Citroën to the west. The planned Parc de Bercy to the east will complete the historic axis of green spaces along the Seine stretching from the Tuileries and Invalides to the Champ-de-Mars and Trocadéro.

Garden-making, like other art forms, draws on the past as it looks to the future. Tradition and innovation are the warp and weft of its history. A garden design is a visual statement of the relationship among human

Garden journalism has flourished since the days of Loudon's *The Gardener's Magazine* (1826–44) and specialized garden shows have become commonplace. The Dresden International Garden Show of 1887, where amateurs and professionals exhibited on public pleasure grounds, carried on the German tradition of the local *Gartenschau*. London's Chelsea Garden Show, first held in 1913 under the aegis of the Royal Horticultural Society, is one of the highlights of the European garden calendar. Today, horticultural societies not only sponsor shows but hold meetings, organize lectures, and publish their own bulletins and magazines. Garden centers have sprung up everywhere, and even supermarkets have plant departments.

beings, their natural environment, and prevailing cultural values. There will always be a handful of eccentrics with the means to turn their "dream gardens" into reality, and there will always be those so imbued with material success they cannot resist turning their "turf" into a status symbol. As gardeners look to Europe, Islam, and the East for inspiration, their designs for large-scale gardens will reflect an adaptation of these various styles.

But small-scale gardeners, whether they live in urban, suburban, or rural parts of the world, share a common goal: to create a retreat, however limited in space or charm, that offers sanctuary from the tensions of modern life, a place where people can once again relate to nature and feel the pulse of our living, growing planet.

From ancient times to the present day, human beings have coaxed private worlds of peace and tranquillity from plots of earth. No two gardens are alike, but all gardeners, like this man planting seeds in terracotta pots (below), have performed the same tasks for millennia with unchanging concentration and delight. Their dream is timeless.

Overleaf: Little Sparta, the garden of sculptor Ian Hamilton Finlay, Stonypath, Scotland.

DOCUMENTS

God *Almightie* first Planted a *Garden*. And indeed,
it is the Purest of Humane pleasures. It is the Greatest
Refreshment to the Spirits of Man; Without
which, *Buildings* and *Pallaces* are but Grosse
Handy-works: And a Man shall ever see,
that when Ages grow to Civility and Elegancie,
Men come to *Build Stately*, sooner then to
Garden Finely: As if *Gardening* were
the Greater Perfection.

Francis Bacon, "Of Gardens," 1625

The Origins of European Gardens

European gardens have roots reaching back not only to the Bible and its mythic Garden of Eden, but to ancient Greece, where sculpture graced sacred groves dedicated to the gods. Greeks are credited with the prototypical "romantic" landscape, and it was through their influence that garden art reached a high-water mark during the Roman empire. Garden philosophy and practice have evolved in the shadow of the Greeks ever since.

The Creation of Paradise on Earth

The Bible describes how God planted Eden, the first garden, and created Adam, the first man—and gardener.

This is the history of the heavens and the earth when they were created,… before any plant of the field was in the earth and before any herb of the field had grown. For the Lord God had not caused it to rain on the earth, and there was no man to till the ground; but a mist went up from the earth and watered the whole face of the ground. And the Lord God formed man of the dust of the ground, and breathed into his nostrils the breath of life; and man became a living being.

The Lord God planted a garden eastward in Eden, and there He put the man whom He had formed. And out of the ground the Lord God made every tree grow that is pleasant to the sight and good for food. The tree of life was also in the midst of the garden, and the tree of the knowledge of good and evil. Now a river went out of Eden to water the garden, and from there it parted and

became four riverheads. The name of the first is Pishon; it is the one which encompasses the whole land of Havilah, where there is gold. And the gold of that land is good. Bdellium and the onyx stone are there. The name of the second river is Gihon; it is the one which encompasses the whole land of Cush. The name of the third river is Hiddekel; it is the one which goes toward the east of Assyria. The fourth river is the Euphrates. Then the Lord God took the man and put him in the garden of Eden to tend and keep it. And the Lord God commanded the man, saying, "Of every tree of the garden you may freely eat; but of the tree of the knowledge of good and evil you shall not eat, for in the day that you eat of it you shall surely die."

Genesis 2:4–17

The Garden of Eden

The blind English poet John Milton wrote his masterly epic poem Paradise Lost *in 1667. His description of Nature's infancy interweaves biblical and classical allusions with philosophical speculation about freedom and one's relationship with the undefiled natural world.*

So on he fares, and to the border comes
Of *Eden*, where delicious Paradise,
Now nearer, Crowns with her enclosure green,
As with a rural mound the champain head
Of a steep wilderness, whose hairie sides
With thicket overgrown, grottesque and wild,
Access deni'd;…

          …in this pleasant soil
His farr more pleasant Garden God ordaind;
Out of the fertil ground he caus'd to grow

Opposite: A Persian paradise garden carved in relief into the palace of Ashurbanipal, Nineveh; and above: the paradise garden metamorphosed into a Christian myth.

All Trees of noblest kind for sight, smell, taste;
And all amid them stood the Tree of Life,
High eminent, blooming Ambrosial Fruit
Of vegetable Gold; and next to Life
Our Death the Tree of Knowledge grew fast by,
Knowledge of Good bought dear by knowing ill.

Southward through *Eden* went a River large,
Nor chang'd his course, but through the shaggie hill
Pass'd underneath ingulft, for God had thrown
That Mountain as his Garden mould high rais'd
Upon the rapid current, which through veins
Of porous Earth with kindly thirst up drawn,
Rose a fresh Fountain, and with many a rill
Waterd the Garden;…
And now divided into four main Streams,
Runs divers, wandring many a famous Realm
And Country whereof here needs no account,
But rather to tell how, if Art could tell,
How from that Saphire Fount the crisped Brooks,
Rowling on Orient Pearl and sands of Gold,
With mazie error under pendant shades
Ran Nectar, visiting each plant, and fed
Flowrs worthy of Paradise which not nice Art
In Beds and curious Knots, but Nature boon
Powrd forth profuse on Hill and Dale and Plain,
Both where the morning Sun first warmly smote
The open field, and where the unpierc't shade
Imbrownd the noontide Bowrs: Thus was this place,
A happy rural seat of various view.

John Milton
Paradise Lost, 1667
Book IV, 131–37, 214–68

A Greek Garden

Many a garden in ancient Rome was inspired by the rustic simplicity of the garden of Alcinous, as described by Homer. Olive trees, fruit trees, and vineyards flourished there in all seasons.

On the outside of the courtyard and next the doors is his orchard, a great one, four land measures, with a fence driven all around it, and there is the place where his fruit trees are grown tall and flourishing, pear trees and pomegranate trees and apple trees with their shining fruit, and the sweet fig trees and the flourishing olive. Never is the fruit spoiled on these, never does it give out, neither in winter time nor summer, but always the West Wind blowing on the fruits brings some to ripeness while he starts others. Pear matures on pear in that place, apple upon apple, grape cluster on grape cluster, fig upon fig. There also he has a vineyard planted that gives abundant produce, some of it a warm area on level ground where the grapes are left to dry

Greek drinking cup from the 5th century BC.

in the sun, but elsewhere they are gathering others and trampling out yet others, and in front of these are unripe grapes that have cast off their bloom while others are darkening. And there at the bottom strip of the field are growing orderly rows of greens, all kinds, and these are lush through the seasons; and there two springs distribute water, one through all the garden space, and one on the other side jets out by the courtyard door, and the lofty house, where townspeople come for their water. Such are the glorious gifts of the gods at the house of Alkinoös.

Homer
The Odyssey, VII, 112–32

A Philosopher's Garden

Some Roman philosophers idealized country life. For them, gardening was a moral imperative.

My garden does not whet the appetite; it satisfies it. It does not provoke thirst through heedless indulgence, but slakes it by proffering its natural remedy. Amid pleasures such as these have I grown old.

Epicurus
4th century BC

A Roman Tombstone

This anonymous epitaph for a humble Roman gardener expresses universal thoughts about a timeless craft.

Accept this graybeard, our Mother Earth!
He practiced a noble craft into ripe old
    age:
Planted olive trees, that you might have
    shade;
Hung vines from elms; and advanced in
    years
Sweetened his breath with anise and
    thyme

And sowed enriching wheat upon the
    plain.
The sluices he opened every morn
    caused
Babbling liquid to overspread your
    bosom,
That orchards might flourish and black-
    barked
Orange trees might bear succulent fruit.
For all he did, welcome him and suffer
    the grass
And wildflowers and moss to overspread
    his grave.

The Villas of Pliny the Younger

The Roman statesman's detailed descriptions of his two villas not only immortalized the gardens he loved so well, but left their imprint on the entire history of garden-making.

My Laurentian place…is large enough for my needs but not expensive to keep up. It opens into a hall, unpretentious but not without dignity, and then there are two colonnades…which enclose a small but pleasant courtyard. This makes a splendid retreat in bad weather, being protected by windows and still more by the overhanging roof.… [On the ground floor] is a dining-room where nothing is known of a high sea but the sound of the breakers, and even that as a dying murmur; it looks on to the garden and the encircling drive.

All round the drive runs a hedge of box, or rosemary to fill any gaps, for box will flourish extensively where it is sheltered by the buildings, but dries up if exposed in the open to the wind and salt spray even at a distance. Inside the inner ring of the drive is a young and shady vine pergola, where the soil is soft and yielding even to the bare foot. The garden itself is thickly planted with mulberries and figs, trees which the soil bears very well though it is less kind to others.... Here begins a covered arcade. ... In front is a terrace scented with violets. As the sun beats down, the arcade increases its heat by reflection and not only retains the sun but keeps off the north-east wind.... At the far end of the terrace, the arcade, and the garden is a suite of rooms which are really and truly my favorites, for I had them built myself. Here is a sun-parlor facing the terrace on one side, the sea on the other, and the sun on both.... The sea-front gains much from the pleasing variety of the houses built either in groups or far apart; from the sea or shore these look like a number of cities....

The [Tuscan] climate in winter is cold and frosty, and so quite impossible for myrtles and olives and any other trees which will only flourish in a continuous mild temperature, but the laurel can grow and does very well....

The countryside is very beautiful. Picture to yourself a vast amphitheatre such as could only be a work of nature; the great spreading plain is ringed round by mountains, their summits crowned by ancient woods of tall trees, where there is a good deal of mixed hunting to be had.... Below them the vineyards spreading down every slope weave their uniform pattern far and wide, their lower limit bordered by a belt of shrubs.... The meadows are bright with flowers, covered with trefoil and other delicate plants which always seem soft and fresh.... My house is on the lower slopes of a hill but commands as good a view as if it were higher up, for the ground rises so gradually that the slope is imperceptible, and you find yourself at the top without noticing the climb.... It faces mainly south, and so from

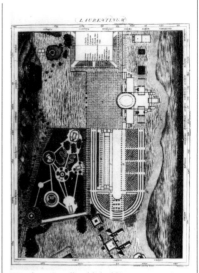

Robert Castell published his reconstructions of Pliny the Younger's villas in 1728.

midday onwards (a little earlier in winter) it seems to invite the sun into the colonnade....

In front of the colonnade is a terrace laid out with box hedges clipped into different shapes, from which a bank slopes down, also with figures of animals cut out of box facing each other on either side. On the level below there waves—or I might have said ripples—a bed of acanthus. All round is a path hedged by bushes which are trained and cut into different shapes, and then a drive, oval like a racecourse, inside which are various box figures and clipped dwarf shrubs. The whole garden is enclosed by a dry-stone wall which is hidden from sight by a box hedge planted in tiers; outside is a meadow, as well worth seeing for its natural beauty as the formal garden I have described; then fields and many

O pposite: the "seaside" Laurentian Villa; above: the "country" Tuscan Villa.

more meadows and woods....

The center [of the riding-ground] is quite open so that the whole extent of the course can be seen as one enters. It is planted round with ivy-clad plane trees, green with their own leaves above, and below with the ivy which climbs over trunk and branch and links tree to tree as it spreads across them.... Roses grow there and the cool shadow alternates with the pleasant warmth of the sun.... Between the grass lawns here there are box shrubs clipped into innumerable shapes, some being letters which spell the gardener's name or his master's; small obelisks of box alternate with fruit trees, and then suddenly in the midst of this ornamental scene is what looks like a piece of rural country planted there.

The Letters of the Younger Pliny
Book II, 17, and Book V, 6

Virgil: Poet and Botanist

Virgil's Georgics, *a lengthy poem about agriculture, was not only a master-piece of Latin verse, but for medieval gardeners and farmers an indispensable practical guide.*

Indeed, if I were not now near the end
Of work, in haste to furl the sails and
   turn
The prow toward land, I'd sing of all the
   care
We spend on dressing fertile garden-
   plots,
Of Paestum's roses blooming twice a
   year,
Of riversides where endive loves to
   drink,
Of green-banked celery, how the curling
   gourd
Swells out its paunch and winds off into
   grass;
Nor would I fail to mention the
   narcissus
Flowering late, the curved acanthus'
   stem,
Pale ivy, and the myrtles' love of shores.
For I recall the towers of Tarentum,
Where black Galaesus waters yellow
   fields:
There once I saw an old man from
   Corycia,
With a patch of unclaimed land allotted
   him,
Not suitable for pasture, crops, or wine.
This farmer, spacing herbs among his
   thickets,
And setting out white lilies, slender
   poppies,
And vervain, felt sure that his riches
   matched
The wealth of kings, when he came
   home at night
And heaped his table high with
   unbought foods.

He plucked the first Spring rose, the
first Fall fruits;
And when the sullen Winter still hung
on,
Bursting rocks with cold, and reining in
With ice the running streams, he went
to clip
Soft strands of hyacinth and railed aloud
At Summer's tardy pace and the laggard
winds.
His bees increased, his swarms were the
most prolific,
He first drew honey foam from his
close-packed hives.
His lime trees were luxuriant, like his
pines:
For every orchard blossom in the Spring
The ripe trees bore a fruit at harvest
time.
He set in rows his elms when well
along,
Pear trees already hard, and blackthorn
sloes,
Planes large enough to offer drinkers
shade.

Virgil
The Georgics, IV, 116–48

Advice from a Roman Specialist

Lucius Junius Moderatus Columella's De
Re Rustica *is a twelve-volume treatise on
agriculture and practical gardening.*

But when bright Zephyr with his sun-
warmed breeze
Thaws the Riphaean winter's numbing
frost,
And Orpheus' Lyre deserts the starry
pole
And dives into the deep, and swallows
hail
Spring's advent at their nests, the
gardener
Should with rich mould or asses' solid
dung

Or other ordure glut the starving
earth....
Now let him with the hoe's well-
sharpened edge
Again attack the earth's surface packed
with rain
And hard with frost; then with the
tooth of rake
Or broken mattock mix the living turf
With clods of earth and all the
crumbling wealth
Of the ripe field set free; then let him
take
The shining hoe, worn by the soil, and
trace
Straight, narrow ridges from the
opposing bounds
And these across with narrow paths
divide.
Now when the earth, its clear divisions
marked
As with the comb, shining, from squalor
free,
Shall claim her seeds, 'tis time to paint
the earth
With varied flowers, like stars brought
down from heaven,
White snow-drops and the yellow-
shining eyes
Of marigolds and fair narcissus-blooms,
Fierce lions' gaping mouths and the
white cups
Of blooming lilies and the hyacinths,
Snow-white or blue. Then let the violet
Be planted, which lies pale upon the
ground
Or blooms with gold and purple
blossoms crowned,
Likewise the rose too full of maiden
blush.
Next scatter all-heal with its saving tear,
And celandines with their health-giving
juice,
And poppies which will bind elusive
sleep;

Let onion's fruitful seed from Megara
come,
Which sharpen men's desires and fit
them for the girls,
And those which Sicca gathers, hidden
deep
Beneath Gaetulian clods and colewort,
too,
Which, sown beside Priapus rich in
fruits,
May rouse up sluggish husbands to
make love.
Next lowly chervil plant and succory
Welcome to jaded palates, lettuce too
With fibers soft, garlic with much-cleft
heads,
Wide-scented leeks, and all that a
skilled cook
Mixes with beans to make a laborer's
meal....
Now is the time, if pickles cheap you
seek,
To plant the caper and harsh elecampane
And threatening fennel; creeping roots
of mint
And fragrant flowers of dill are spaced
now
And rue, which the Palladian berry's
taste
Improves, and mustard which will make
him weep,
Whoe'er provokes it; now the roots are
set
Of alexanders dark, the weepy onion,
Likewise the herb which seasons
draughts of milk
And will remove the brand, signal of
flight,
From brows of runagates, and, by its
name
In the Greek tongue, its virtue
demonstrates.

Lucius Junius Moderatus Columella
De Re Rustica
Book X, 86–126

The Ancients Revisited

*The poet and gardener Alexander Pope
helped lay the ideological groundwork for
English garden design in the 18th century
as opposed to formal French gardens. A
devoted classicist, he translated into
English Homer's description of the
garden of Alcinous.*

There is certainly something in the
amiable Simplicity of unadorned
Nature, that spreads over the Mind a
more noble sort of Tranquility, and a
loftier Sensation of Pleasure, than can
be raised from the nicer Scenes of Art.

This was the Taste of the Ancients
in the Gardens.... The two most celebrated Wits of the World have each of
them left us a particular Picture of a
Garden; wherein those great Masters,
being wholly unconfined, and Painting
at Pleasure, may be thought to have
given a full Idea of what they esteemed
most excellent in this way. These (one
may observe) consist intirely of the
useful Part of Horticulture, Fruit-Trees,
Herbs, Water, *&c.* The Pieces I am
speaking of are *Virgil*'s Account of the
Garden of the old *Corycian*, and
Homer's of that of *Alcinous*....

How contrary to this Simplicity is the
modern Practice of Gardening; we seem
to make it our Study to recede from
Nature, not only in the various Tonsure
of Greens into the most regular and
formal Shapes, but even in monstrous
Attempts beyond the reach of the Art
itself.... I believe it is no wrong
Observation, that Persons of Genius,
and those who are most capable of Art,
are always most fond of Nature, as such
are chiefly sensible, that all Art consists
in the Imitation and Study of Nature.

Alexander Pope
"On Verdant Sculpture," 1713

Gardens of the Middle Ages

The medieval garden served as both a Christian allegory and a literary place of carnal love and earthly delight. It was almost always walled, as described in the literature of the time, and divided into square or rectangular plots.

A poet at work in his garden, from a medieval French manuscript.

The Sacred Garden

The medieval hortus conclusus, symbolizing the Church and the purity of the Virgin Mary, can be traced to the garden in the lyrical Song of Solomon.

A garden inclosed is my sister, my spouse; a spring shut up, a fountain sealed. Thy plants are an orchard of pomegranates, with pleasant fruits; camphire, with spikenard, spikenard and saffron; calamus and cinnamon, with all trees of frankincense; myrrh and aloes, with all the chief spices: A fountain of gardens, a well of living waters, and streams from Lebanon.

Awake, O north wind; and come, thou south; blow upon my garden, that the spices thereof may flow out. Let my beloved come into his garden, and eat his pleasant fruits.

I am come into my garden, my sister, my spouse: I have gathered my myrrh with my spice; I have eaten my honeycomb with my honey; I have drunk my wine with my milk: eat, O friends; drink, yea, drink abundantly, O beloved.

The Song of Solomon 4:12–16, 5:1

The Garden of Earthly Delight

Eden is the prototype of the hortus deliciarum, symbol of earthly pleasure.

The garden was surrounded, not by wall or fence but only by air. Through black magic, the garden was enclosed by air on all sides as if it were enclosed by iron, so that nothing could enter there except at one particular entrance. All summer and winter, flowers and ripe fruit were plentiful there. Such a spell was on the fruit that it could be eaten inside but not taken outside. Whoever wanted to carry some outside would never know the way out, for he would not find the exit until he returned the fruit to its place. Among the birds that fly under heaven, charming and delighting men with their joyous song, every single one could be heard there, and there were several of every species. As far as the land stretched, it bore every spice and medicinal herb effective in any kind of treatment, for everything had been planted there and was found in abundance.

Chrétien de Troyes
Erec et Enide, c. 1165–90

The Romance of the Rose

This dream poem is an allegorical warning of the dangers of profane love. The poet dreams that he is walking along a river when he discovers an enchanted enclosed garden. He is greeted by a beautiful woman, Oiseuse, or Idleness.

At this point I left there and went off alone to enjoy myself here and there throughout the garden.… The garden was a completely straight, regular square, as long as it was wide.… There was no tree which might bear fruit of which there were not one or two, or perhaps more, in the garden. There were apple trees, I remember well, that bore pomegranates, an excellent food for the sick. There was a great abundance of nut trees that in their season bore such fruit as nutmegs, which are neither bitter nor insipid. There were almond trees, and many fig and date trees were planted in the garden. He who needed to could find many a good spice there, cloves, licorice, fresh grains of paradise, zedoary, anise, cinnamon, and many a delightful spice good to eat after meals. There were the domestic garden fruit trees,… and the garden was thronged with large laurels and tall pines, with

olive trees and cypresses, of which there are scarcely any here. There were enormous branching elms and, along with them, hornbeams and beech trees, straight hazels, aspen and ash, maples, tall firs, and oaks.… Know too that these trees were spaced out as they should be; one was placed at a distance of more than five or six fathoms from another. The branches were long and high and, to keep the place from heat, were so thick above that the sun could not shine on the earth or harm the tender grass for even one hour.…

In places there were clear fountains, without water insects or frogs and shaded by the trees.… In little brooks, which Diversion had made there as channels, the water ran along down, making a sweet and pleasing murmur. Along the brooks and the banks of the clear, lively fountains, sprang the thick, short grass. There one could couch his mistress as though on a feather bed, for the earth was sweet and moist on account of the fountains, since as much grass as possible grew there.

But the thing that most improved the place was the appearance that, winter and summer, there was always an abundance of flowers. There were very beautiful violets, fresh, young periwinkles; there were white and red flowers, and wonderful yellow ones. The earth was very artfully decorated and painted with flowers of various colors and sweetest perfumes.

I won't offer you a long fable about this pleasant, delectable place, and it is now time for me to stop, for I could not recall all of the beauty and great delight of the garden.

Guillaume de Lorris and Jean de Meung
Le Roman de la Rose
c. 1235–80

The Renaissance

The Ancients were resurrected and given a new lease on life in the 15th and 16th centuries.

The Dream of Poliphilus

Allusions to classical literature and mythology abound in Francesco Colonna's seminal Hypnerotomachia Poliphili (Dream of Poliphilus), *illustrated with peculiar little woodcuts, which were to influence Renaissance gardens throughout Europe.*

And rounde about this pleasant place,… a little Channel comming by a sluce from the Bridge, entering in and unlading it selfe, was the cause of a goodly faire Poole, broad and large, in a verie good order, trimmed about and beautified with a fence of sweete Roses and Gessamine. … And from thence beholding the plaine fieldes, it was wonderfull to see the greennes thereof, powdered with such varietie of sundrie sorted colours, and divers fashioned floures,…that they did greatly comfort mee (having lost my selfe) but even with the looking uppon them…. In a convenient order and sweete disposed sort by a just line, grew the greene and sweete smelling Orenges, Lymons, Citrons, Pomegranettes,…laden with the aboundance of their floure and fruites, breathing forth a most sweet and delectable odoriferous smell…. For which cause I stood amazed and in great doubt what to thinke or doo, and the rather because in that place I had seene such a marveilous fountaine, the varietie of hearbes, the colours of floures, the placing orderly of the trees, the faire and commodious disposition of the seat, the sweet chirpings and quiet singing of Birds, and the temperate and healthful ayre…. And somewhat I was grieved that I could no longer abide in such a place where so many delightful sightes did present themselves unto mee.

Francesco Colonna
Hypnerotomachia Poliphili, 1499
trans. Sir Robert Darllington, 1592

The woodcuts published in *Hypnerotomachia Poliphili* (1499) inspired many Renaissance gardeners.

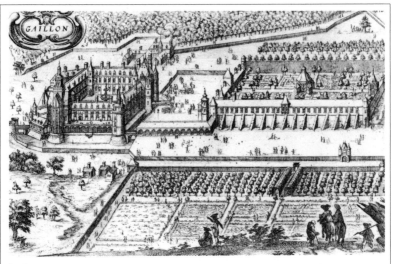

The chateau of Gaillon was an early example of Renaissance influence on French architecture.

Montaigne's Travels in Italy

The grand tour was an indispensable part of every well-bred European's education and culture.

Tivoli.... Here are to be seen that famous palace and garden of the cardinal of Ferrara: it is a very beautiful thing, but incomplete in many parts, and the work is not being continued by the present cardinal. Here I examined everything most particularly. I would try to describe it here, but there are published books and pictures on the subject. The gushing of an infinity of jets of water checked and launched by a single spring that can be worked from far off, I had seen elsewhere on my trip, both at Florence and at Augsburg, as has been stated above. The music of the organ, which is real music and a natural organ, though always playing the same thing, is effected by means of the water, which falls with great violence into a round arched cave and agitates the air that is in there and forces it, in order to get out, to go through the pipes of the organ and supply it with wind. Another stream of water, driving a wheel with certain teeth on it, causes the organ keyboard to be struck in a certain order; so you hear an imitation of the sound of trumpets. In another place you hear the song of birds, which are little bronze flutes that you see at regals; they give a sound like those little earthenware pots full of water that little children blow into by the spout, this by an artifice like that of the organ; and then by other springs they set in motion an owl, which, appearing at the top of the rock, makes this harmony cease instantly, for the birds are frightened by his presence; and then he leaves the place to them again. This goes on alternately as long as you want.

Elsewhere there issues a noise as of cannon shots; elsewhere a more frequent smaller noise, as of harquebus shots. This is done by a sudden fall of water into channels; and the air, laboring at the same time to get out, engenders this noise. All these inventions, or similar ones, produced by these same natural causes, I have seen elsewhere.

Michel de Montaigne
Travel Journal, 1580–1

Francis Bacon's Garden Calendar

The famous lord chancellor, philosopher, and scientist paints a picture of an ideal garden where spring would be perpetual despite London's climate.

I doe hold it, in the Royall Ordering of *Gardens*, there ought to be *Gardens*, for all the *Moneths* in the Yeare: In which, severally, Things of Beautie, may be then in Season. For *December*, and *January*, and the Latter Part of *November*, you must take such Things, as are Greene all Winter: Holly; Ivy; Bayes; Juniper; Cipresse Trees; Eugh; Pine-Apple-Trees; Firre-Trees; Rose-Mary; Lavander; Periwinckle, the White, the Purple, and the Blewe; Germander; Flagges; Orange-Trees; Limon-trees; and Mirtles, if they be stooved; & Sweet Marjoram warme set. There followeth, for the latter Part of *January*, and *February*, the Mezerion Tree, which then blossomes; Crocus Vernus, both the Yellow, and the Gray; Prime-Roses; Anemones; The Early Tulippa; Hiacynthus Orientalis; Chamairis; Frettellaria. For *March*, There come Violets, specially the Single Blew, which are the Earliest; The Yellow Daffadill; The Dazie; The Almond-Tree in Blossome; The Peach-Tree in Blossome; The Cornelian-Tree in Blossome; Sweet-Briar. In *April* follow, The Double white Violet; The Wall-flower; The Stock-Gilly-Flower; The Couslip; Flower-De-lices, & Lillies of all Natures; Rose-mary Flowers; The Tulippa; The Double Piony; the Pale Daffadill; The French Honny-Suckle; The Cherry-Tree in Blossome; The Dammasin, and Plum-Trees in Blossome; The White-Thorne in Leafe; The Lelacke Tree. In *May*, and *June*, come Pincks of all sorts, Specially the Blush Pincke; Roses of all kinds, except the Muske, which comes later; Hony-Suckles; Strawberries; Buglosse; Columbine; The French Mary-gold; Flos Africanus; Cherry-Tree in Fruit; Ribos; Figges in Fruit; Raspes; Vine Flowers; Lavender in Flowers;… In *July*, come Gilly-Flowers of all Varieties; Muske Roses; The Lime-Tree in blossome; Early Peares, and Plummes in Fruit; Ginnitings, Quadlins. In *August*, come Plummes of all sorts in Fruit; Peares; Apricockes; Berberies; Filberds; Musk-Melons; Monks Hoods, of all colours. In *September*, come Grapes; Apples; Poppies of all colours; Peaches; Melo-Cotones; Nectarines; Cornelians; Wardens; Quinces. In *October*, and the beginning of *November*, come Services; Medlars; Bullises, Roses Cut or Removed to come late; Hollyokes; and such like. These Particulars are for the *Climate* of *London*, But my meaning is Perceived, that you may have *Ver Perpetuum*, as the Place affords.

Sir Francis Bacon
"Of Gardens," 1625

The Belvedere Court

Georgina Masson lived for many years in Italy in the converted stables of a historic Roman villa. Her classic book on the gardens of Italy remains a landmark work in the field of garden design.

[The design for the Belvedere Court] resulted in a revolution in garden design that changed the whole conception of gardens in Italy and ultimately in Europe.... Probably shortly after his election to the Papacy in 1503, Julius II transferred part at least of his collection of sculpture to the Vatican, and it seems likely that from the first he entertained the idea of using Innocent VIII's old Villa Belvedere for the display of works of art in the classical style. Though admirably sited, both according to the old Roman concepts and the tenets of Alberti, the Belvedere stood at some distance from the Papal palace and was separated from it by a rising stretch of open ground.... It was probably this shortcoming that first inspired Julius with the idea of connecting the Belvedere to the palace and from that it was but a short step, given the grandeur of the Pope's ideas and the currents of thought at the time, to a project for creating a garden in the style of an ancient Roman villa.

Fortunately there was already living in Rome the architect who was best qualified to put Julius' ideas into effect. This was Donato Bramante.... The general requirements of Bramante's commission were—first to provide a sheltered means of access from the Vatican Palace to the Villa Belvedere which was slightly out of line with the Papal apartments in the palace and separated from them by a wide stretch of rising ground; second, to create a setting worthy of the Pope's collection of sculpture; and third to design a garden that contained a theatre and provided a suitable stage for the

pageantry of the Papal Court as well as a private retreat for a humanist pope of the Renaissance. This was no small order in a world whose conception of gardens was still little advanced from the *hortus conclusus* of medieval times.... The Belvedere court was no mere collection of antique motifs pieced together by a virtuoso, but a conception unique in its day, that related ancient art to the current trends in the study of perspective in painting, thereby introducing the vital third dimension into garden design. As a result, the level enclosed garden room of the Tuscan humanists gave way before the new-old Roman conception of moulding the terrain to an architectural form, axially related to the building of which it was an adjunct, linking this to the surrounding landscape (though not yet merging into it) and opening the whole layout to the horizons of the outside world.

Briefly the synthesis of Bramante's plan was the enclosure of the area within the axis of the palace and the Belvedere by two vast loggias, triple at their lowest level, double and finally single as they coincided with the series of terraces by whose creation he gave a definite architectural form to the hill.... But the most revolutionary part of Bramante's design was his treatment of the terraces on the far side of the theatre—here was no timid series of enclosed garden rooms but a magnificent perspective achieved by the use of monumental stairs and ramps that linked the terraces and rose to a climax in a niche approached by a semicircular series of steps at the far end.

With this one plan Bramante dictated the basis of European garden design for more than two centuries to come.

Georgina Masson
Italian Gardens, 1961

The Royal Gardens of France

Nicolas Fouquet may have made a fatal misjudgment when he presented his spectacular new gardens to the young Louis XIV, but this challenge, as the king saw it, soon transformed the landscape of France and made her royal gardens the envy of Europe. Limitless vistas mirrored the aspirations of France's monarchy.

The Party that Changed the Face of a Country

When Louis Le Vau, André Le Nôtre, and Charles Le Brun had completed the gardens commissioned by Fouquet, minister of finance to Louis XIV, Fouquet decided to throw himself a party.

The air was filled with the sound of a thousand fountains falling into marvellously fashioned basins, "as if it were the throne of Neptune," as a contemporary put it. Louis advanced down the central walk towards the canal between walls of water from a hundred jets. He looked at the garden from every point of view. After a sumptuous supper, Molière's *Les Facheux* was performed on the steps of the Grille d'Eau. Moliére appeared in his everyday clothes affecting to be taken by surprise, saying that he had no actors and no time to prepare the entertainment that was apparently expected, unless some unforseen help was forthcoming. He

Some of the many garden enclosures that dotted Versailles were more secluded than others; but they all lent themselves to recreation, banquets, and outdoor entertainment.

begged the king to order the spectacle to begin. Thereupon a shell opened, revealing a Naiad who delivered a prologue; trees came to life, statues walked and the spectacle proceeded. When night had fallen lanterns placed along the cornices of the chateau made it seem ablaze. The grotto was lit up; and suddenly from the grass amphitheatre beyond, a display of rockets shot into the air, forming figures of fleurs-de-lys and other devices above the heads of the spectators; while a whale advanced down the canal, discharging fireworks to the accompaniment of drums and trumpets, as if a furious battle were being fought. When all was apparently over, and the king was returning to the chateau, more rockets, fired from the dome, covered the whole of the garden with a vault of fire.… On 5 September, Fouquet arrived at the chateau… unaware that his disgrace was imminent. He was arrested as he left, outside the castle precincts, by D'Artagnan, an officer of La Compagnie des Mousquetaires.… The charges were high treason and embezzlement.

Kenneth Woodbridge
Princely Gardens, 1986

Louis Transforms a Hunting Lodge

Inspired—and enraged—by the splendor of Fouquet's gardens, Louis XIV began work on a small lodge at Versailles.

So the garden becomes the setting for the great royal fête.… It was the ritual function of those vast entertainments to embody in the king those cosmic powers and virtues, those ideas, of which he was normally simply the terrestrial reflection. In them, for example, Louis XIV was presented as the Sun King.… At Versailles the whole canopy of sky spreads that Sun in majesty over the garden, while the fountains themselves dance the cosmic nature of the king. The iconography is simple. It is the mother of Apollo, Latona, whom we see at the foot of the stairs; it is Apollo himself who is rising out of the water in the distance (rising out of the west, unfortunately, but that can't be helped). So Louis is, in fact, the whole sky and Apollo as well.

It is when the fountains go on that we can feel a little bit how those great masques must have worked, those illusionistic festivals with their boats, their floats, their fireworks, and their *jets d'eau,* translating the elements into the king. Because, as the fountains rise up, Apollo really seems to be moving. The powerful white jets leaping up before him are a narrative or sculptural embodiment of his action. They make us feel him moving forward in space; they embody his resolution and his power. At the Fountain of Latona, the ballet begins as the jets of water start up out of the mouths of those unfortunate Boeotian peasants who were ill-advised enough to deride Latona and her son and were punished by Zeus by being turned into lizards and frogs. They are the citizens of Paris, who insulted Louis and his mother during the disorders of the Fronde. The water is their cry, and it rises as their anguish mounts to surround Latona at last in an aureole of light like fire. All the elements of that typical four-part, simplified iconography that was used over and over again at Versailles are present: Louis becomes, in fact, earth, air, water, and fire.

Vincent Scully
Architecture: The Natural and the Manmade, 1991

Art or Nature?

The formal garden went out of fashion, and in the 18th century a new spirit of freedom was in the air. The French Revolution signaled the demise of the Ancien Régime *and the dawn of the modern era all across Europe. Gardens were conceived as paintings; painters became gardeners; a queen fancied herself a shepherdess; a young Corsican, an emperor. Gardens ran the gamut from neoclassical to informal to eclectic. Garden design, like leisure and the social order, was in the throes of democratization.*

The Advent of the Landscape Garden

Joseph Addison, a leading advocate of picturesque gardening, set forth the movement's ideology and agenda in an article for The Spectator. *The Englishman's views regarding our response to the natural landscape—a variation on John Locke's theory on the human mind—made a forceful argument for freedom in the age of French absolutism.*

If we consider the Works of *Nature* and *Art*, as they are qualified to entertain the Imagination, we shall find the last very defective, in Comparison of the former; for though they may sometimes appear as Beautiful or Strange, they can have nothing in them of that Vastness and Immensity, which afford so great an Entertainment to the Mind of the Beholder. The one may be as Polite and Delicate as the other, but can never shew her self so August and Magnificent in the Design. There is something more bold and masterly in the rough careless Strokes of Nature, than in the nice Touches and Embellishments of Art. The Beauties of the most stately Garden or Palace lie in a narrow Compass, the

The tomb of Jean-Jacques Rousseau at Ermenonville.

Imagination immediately runs them over, and requires something else to gratifie her; but, in the wide Fields of Nature, the Sight wanders up and down without Confinement, and is fed with an infinite variety of Images, without any certain Stint or Number. For this Reason we always find the Poet in love with a Country-Life, where Nature appears in the greatest Perfection, and furnishes out all those Scenes that are most apt to delight the Imagination....

But tho' there are several of these wild Scenes, that are more delightful than any artificial Shows; yet we find the Works of Nature still more pleasant, the more they resemble those of Art: For in this case our Pleasure rises from a double principle; from the Agreeableness of the Objects to the Eye, and from their Similitude to other Objects.

Joseph Addison
The Spectator, 25 June 1712

Jean-Jacques Rousseau

An early spokesman for informal gardening, Rousseau decried not only French formality but England's plethora of ornamental garden buildings and the Dutch obsession with flowers.

With ecstasy I began to wander through the orchard...I found those [plants] natural to the country, laid out and combined in a way to produce a more cheerful and agreeable effect.... I saw a thousand dazzling wild flowers, among which my eye with surprise distinguished some garden flowers, which seemed to grow naturally with the others.... In the more open spots, here and there and without order and without symmetry,... I followed winding and irregular walks bordered by these flowery thickets and covered with a thousand garlands of woody vines....

"You see nothing laid out in a line, nothing made level," [said Monsieur de Wolmar]. "The carpenter's line never entered this place. Nature plants nothing by the line. The simulated irregularities of the winding paths are artfully managed in order to prolong the walk, hide the edges of the island, and enlarge its apparent size, without creating inconvenient and excessively frequent turnings."

Considering all this, I found it rather curious that they should take so much trouble to hide that very trouble which they had taken. Would it not have been better to have taken none at all?

"In spite of all you have been told," Julie answered me, "you are judging the work by the effect, and you deceive yourself. All that you see are wild or sturdy plants, which need only to be put into the ground and which then come up by themselves.... Those who love nature and cannot go seek it so far away are reduced to doing it violence, to forcing it in some manner to come dwell with them, and all this cannot be effected without a little illusion."

At these words, a thought came to me which made them laugh. "I picture to myself," I said, "a rich man of Paris or London, master of this house, bringing with him an architect who is paid dearly to spoil nature. With what disdain he would enter this simple and rude place! With what contempt he would have all these worthless things torn out! The fine lines he would trace! The fine walks he would cut open! Fine [goose-feet], fine trees shaped like parasols or fans! Fine, well-carved trellises! Fine hedges, well designed, well squared, well contoured!

Temple au Dieu Pan.

The ornamental garden buildings that mushroomed in landscape parks during the 18th century ran the stylistic gamut from classically inspired temples (above) and simulated ruins to rustic huts, Chinese pagodas and bridges, and Turkish tents.

Beautiful grass plots of fine English grass—round, square, crescent-shaped, oval! Fine yew trees, trimmed in the shape of dragons, pagodas, grotesque figures, all sorts of monsters! Fine bronze vases, fine stone fruit with which he would adorn his garden!…"

"When all that shall have been carried out," said Monsieur de Wolmar, "he shall have made a very fine place in which people will hardly ever walk and from which they will always leave eagerly in order to seek the country.…"

Jean-Jacques Rousseau
La Nouvelle Héloïse, 1761

Goethe Plans an English Garden

In Goethe's novel Die Wahlverwandt-schaften (Elective Affinities)*, we meet an aristocratic couple who, like many of their contemporaries during the age of Romanticism in Europe, create a landscape garden that combines ingenuity and intuition.*

Eduard, a wealthy landowner in his early middle years, had been spending the loveliest hour of an April afternoon in his tree nursery, grafting fresh shoots on young stocks just sent him. His task finished, he gathered his tools into their case and was contemplating his work with satisfaction when the gardener approached, pleased by his master's interest and assistance.

"Have you seen my wife, by any chance?" Eduard inquired, just as he was on the point of leaving.

"She is over there on the newly laid out grounds," the gardener replied. "The summer house which she has been building against the rock wall opposite the castle will be finished today. Everything has turned out beautifully and will certainly please Your Grace. The view from there is remarkable; the village is below; a little to the right is the church, whose steeple you can almost look over; and, opposite, the castle and park."

"Quite so," Eduard said. "Not far from here I could see the men working."

"And, then," the gardener went on, "to the right, the valley opens out, and you look over the meadows with their many trees, far into a serene and bright distance. The path up to the rocks has been very prettily laid out. Her Ladyship is ingenious; it is a pleasure to work for her."

"Please go and tell her to wait for me," said Eduard. "Tell her that I should like to see and enjoy her latest achievement."

The gardener hurried away, and Eduard followed after a little while. He walked down the terraces and, in passing, looked into the greenhouses and at the hotbeds. When he came to the brook, he crossed a foot bridge and arrived at a point where the way branched in two directions. He did not take the path which ran across the churchyard in an almost straight line toward the rock wall, but followed the other, which wound gently upward, leading a little farther to the left through pleasant shrubbery. He sat down for a moment, on a bench where the paths rejoined; and then he started the climb which brought him, by a steep and uneven way, over all sorts of steps and ledges, finally to the summer house.

At the door Charlotte welcomed her husband and led him to a seat where he could take in at a single glance, through door and windows, the different views of the landscape, as though set in frames. He was delighted and expressed his hope that spring would soon bring new life to the surroundings....

And so they arrived, over rocks and through bushes and shrubbery at the summit, which was not level but consisted of a succession of grassy ridges. Village and castle, at their back, were no longer visible. Below they saw ponds stretching along the valley, backed by wooded hills; where these ended, steep rocks formed a perpendicular wall behind the last expanse of water, which reflected their magnificent forms on its surface. In a ravine, where a rushing brook poured down into one of the ponds, was a grist-mill; almost hidden among surrounding trees it seemed to offer a pleasant and quiet retreat. In the entire semicircle which they overlooked, a great variety of depths and heights, of thickets and of forests, spread out before them, promising with their early green a future abundant prospect.

Goethe
Elective Affinities, 1809

The Flower Garden

Humphry Repton, whose claim to be "Capability" Brown's successor did not go undisputed, lived to see the advent of eclecticism and the "gardenesque" style.

In the execution of my profession, I have often experienced great difficulty and opposition in attempting to correct the false and mistaken taste for placing a large house in a naked grass-field, without any apparent line of separation between the ground exposed to cattle and the ground annexed to the house, which I consider as peculiarly under the management of art.

This line of separation being admitted, advantage may be easily taken to ornament the lawn with flowers and shrubs, and to attach to the mansion that scene of "embellished neatness," usually called a pleasure-ground.

The quantity of this dressed ground was formerly very considerable. The royal gardens of Versailles, or those of Kensington Palace, when filled with company, want no other animation; but a large extent of ground without moving objects, however neatly kept, is but a melancholy scene. If solitude delight, we seek it rather in the covert of a wood, or the sequestered alcove of a flower-garden, than in the open lawn of an extensive pleasure-ground.

I have therefore frequently been the means of restoring acres of useless garden to the deer or sheep, to which they more properly belong....

To common observers, the most obvious difference between Mr. Brown's style and that of ancient gardens, was the change from straight to waving or serpentine lines. Hence, many of his followers had supposed good taste in gardening to consist in avoiding all lines that are straight or parallel, and in adopting forms which they deem more consonant to nature, without considering what objects were natural and what were artificial.

Humphry Repton
Repton's Landscape Gardening
1840

Et in Arcadia Ego

Tom Stoppard's play Arcadia *takes place on an English estate, Sidley Park, during two different eras: early in the 19th century and late in the 20th. Lady Croom, mistress of the 19th-century home examines with horror the plans of Noakes, the "landskip gardener," to transform her property from the "landscape" to the "picturesque" style; his plans even include the addition of a hermitage complete with living hermit. A century later, Hannah, who is writing a history of the park through the ages, laments the damage wrought by both contrived styles.*

Scene 1: Early in the 19th century

Lady Croom: ...I would not have recognized my own garden but for your ingenious book [a sketch book in the manner of Humphry Repton]—is it not?—look! Here is the park as it appears to us now, and here as it might be when Mr Noakes has done with it. Where there is the familiar pastoral refinement of an Englishman's garden, here is an eruption of gloomy forest and towering crag, of ruins where there was never a house, of water dashing against rocks where there was never neither spring nor a stone I could not throw the length of a cricket pitch. My hyacinth dell is become a haunt for hobgoblins, my Chinese bridge, which I am assured is superior to the one at Kew, and for all I know at Peking, is usurped by a fallen obelisk overgrown with briars...Pray, what is this rustic hovel that presumes to superpose itself on my gazebo?

Noakes: That is the hermitage, madam.

Lady Croom: I am bewildered.

Brice: It is all irregular, Mr Noakes.

Noakes: It is, sir. Irregularity is one of the chiefest principles of the picturesque style—

Lady Croom: But Sidley Park is already a picture, and a most amiable picture too. The slopes are green and gentle. The trees are companionably grouped at intervals that show them to advantage. The rill is a serpentine ribbon unwound from the lake peacably contained by meadows on which the right amount of sheep are tastefully arrranged—in short, it is nature as God intended, and I can say with the painter, "*Et in Arcadia ego!*" "Here I am in Arcadia."

Scene 2: Present day. Two historians discuss how changes in the microcosm of

R epton's planned improvements for Beaudesert in England combined traditional landscape park design principles with innovative lakeside terrace gardens that soon became fashionable.

the gardens over the years have reflected larger changes.

Hannah: The hermit was *placed* in the landscape exactly as one might place a pottery gnome. And there he lived out his life as a garden ornament.

Bernard: Did he do anything?

Hannah: Oh, he was very busy. When he died, the cottage was stacked solid with paper. Hundreds of pages. Thousands. Peacock says he was suspected of genius. It turned out, of course, he was off his head. He'd covered every sheet with cabalistic proofs that the world was coming to an end. It's perfect, isn't it? A perfect symbol, I mean.

Bernard: Oh yes. Of what?

Hannah: The whole Romantic sham, Bernard! It's what happened to the Enlightenment, isn't it? A century of intellectual rigour turned in on itself. A mind in chaos suspected of genius. In a setting of cheap thrills and false emotion. The history of the garden says it all, beautifully. There's an engraving of Sidley Park in 1730 that makes you want to weep. Paradise in the age of reason. By 1760 everything had gone—the topiary, pools and terraces, fountains, an avenue of limes—the whole sublime geometry was ploughed under by Capability Brown. The grass went from the doorstep to the horizon and the best box hedge in Derbyshire was dug up for the ha-ha so that the fools could pretend they were living in God's countryside. And then Richard Noakes came in to bring God up to date. By the time he'd finished it looked like this (*the sketch book*). The decline from thinking to feeling, you see.

Tom Stoppard
Arcadia, 1993

The Diversity of 20th-Century Gardening

Individual choice has been the keynote of 20th-century gardens, yet they mirror the entire history of our civilization. Our identity is woven from many different stylistic threads, and our relationship with nature is as complex and multifaceted as it is essential.

The Wild Garden

In the late 19th century, William Robinson revolutionized garden design by arguing for studied simplicity and encouraging such practices as informal planting and the use of perennials instead of tender exotics.

This term is especially applied to the placing of perfectly hardy exotic plants in places, and under conditions, where they will become established and take care of themselves. It has nothing to do with the old idea of the "wilderness," though it may be carried out in connection with it. It does not necessarily mean the picturesque garden, for a garden may be highly picturesque, and yet in every part be the result of ceaseless care. What it does mean is

One of the Royal Horticultural Society's great glass houses as it appeared in the 19th century.

explained by the Winter Aconite flowering under a grove of naked leaves in February; by the Snowflake growing abundantly in meadows by the Thames side; by the perennial Lupine dyeing an islet with its purple in a Scotch river; and by the Apennine Anemone staining an English wood blue before the blooming of our Bluebells. Multiply these instances a thousand-fold, illustrated by many different types of plants and hardy climbers from countries as cold and colder than our own, and one may get a just idea of the wild garden.

William Robinson
The English Flower Garden, 1883

The Grande Dame of the English Garden

By applying Robinsonian concepts to an architectural framework, Gertrude Jekyll blurred the distinction between formal and informal approaches to gardening. This symbiosis, and her pioneering work with herbaceous borders, were watersheds in 20th-century garden design.

To prevent undue disappointment, those who wish for beautiful flower borders and whose enthusiasm is greater than their knowledge, should be reminded that if a border is to be planted for pictorial effect, it is impossible to maintain that effect and to have the space well filled for any period longer than three months, and that even for such a time there will have to be contrivances such as have been described.

It should also be borne in mind that a good hardy flower border cannot be made all at once.

Gertrude Jekyll
Colour in the Flower Garden
1908

A Gardening Team

Sissinghurst is the most famous and widely imitated postwar garden in England. Vita-Sackville West and her husband Harold Nicolson built up their home and gardens from the virtual rubble of an Elizabethan estate. The gardens were their great delight. Vita oversaw the plantings and Harold concerned himself with the overall architecture of the garden. Vita wrote about them in letters, her poetry, and in a column in The Observer.

Now, look here, Hadji [nickname for Harold], the silver birches—we have been lucky, you say, but was that position for them carefully thought out? —lucky indeed! He always does that— he says: "I say Mar what a bit of luck those orange tulips coming up just where they show in that gap in the Apple Garden"—Lucky, indeed! Monster! I shan't tell you about the honesty and forget-me-not—it is a cloud of pink and blue—if you saw it you would say how lucky it elected to grow together just above the pond.

Letter from Vita Sackville-West
to Harold Nicolson, 3 May 1928

What a perfect day it was yesterday, the pale stream of the River Thames was gilded by the strangest alchemy and all the willows were bursting into green: I sat in my tower looking out towards the Chilterns and thought of our lovely garden all green and yellow and expectant. It is, is, is a lovely garden and I was so happy on Sunday just walking with you among the loveliness you made. I think it is the loveliest garden in the whole world.

Letter from Harold Nicolson
to Vita Sackville-West, 24 April 1951

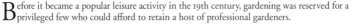

Before it became a popular leisure activity in the 19th century, gardening was reserved for a privileged few who could afford to retain a host of professional gardeners.

There is a nice article about roses in Country Life and quite a lot about our garden…"gardens such as Hidcote, St Nicholas and Sissinghurst Castle"… I think it is funny how our rubbish dump has blundered into fame.

> Letter from Vita Sackville-West
> to Harold Nicolson,
> 29 September 1954

I hope you will survey a low sea of grey clumps of foliage, pierced here and there with tall white flowers. I visualize the white trumpets of dozens of Regale lilies, grown three years ago from seed, coming up through the grey of southernwood and artemisia and cotton-lavender, with grey-and-white edging plants such as *Dianthus* Mrs. Sinkins and the silvery mats of *Stachys lanata*, more familiar and so much nicer under its English name of Rabbits' ears or Saviour's Flannel. There will be white pansies, and white peonies, and white irises with their grey leaves…at least, I hope there will be all these things. I don't want to boast in advance about my grey, green, and white garden. It may be a terrible failure. I wanted only to suggest that such experiments are worth trying, and that you can adapt them to your own taste and your own opportunities.

All the same, I cannot help hoping that the grey ghostly barn-owl will sweep silently across a pale garden, next summer in the twilight—the pale garden that I am now planting, under the first flakes of snow.

Vita Sackville-West
The Observer, January 1950

I wish I could find out who Mme Lauriol was in real life, to have so sumptuous a flower called after her. I suspect that she may have belonged to the *haute cocotterie* of Paris at that date, or possibly I misjudge her and she may have been the perfectly respectable wife of some Mr de Barny, perhaps a rose-grower of Lyon. Someone ought to write the biographies of persons who have had roses named in their honour. Who was Madame Hardy? Who was Charles de Mills? I don't know, and I long for a Who's Who to correct my ignorance.

Vita Sackville-West
The Observer, 25 August 1957

The Education of a Gardener

Like Gertrude Jekyll, Russell Page started out as a painter and architect and went on to become an accomplished garden designer. The elegance of his designs masks the manipulation essential to all garden-making.

Wherever I make my garden the main elements will not change: in front of the house a deliberately composed "landscape," so quietly arranged that one would not tire of it; nearby a working garden; and subsidiary to both of these, such additional features as a landscape, the soil and the site would indicate and as I could afford.… A garden really lives only insofar as it is an expression of faith, the embodiment of a hope and a song of praise.… I will surely have many aims in connection with every garden I attempt; the first perhaps quite simply is to leave a place more beautiful that I find it.… I draw and draw, searching for a composition which will come right in its own time only, perhaps at once, perhaps after hours and days of work. Of course the answer is inherent in the problem.… So now my aim includes my own necessity for clearer thinking.… All these I must remember as I struggle with problems of drawing and composing on paper, with the spadework of calculations and lists, the difficulties of construction, the chance vagaries of behaviour of plants and men, soil and weather for which I have to remember to make allowances.…

When I come to build my own garden it can scarcely take another form than the one which is a reflection of its maker. If I want it to be "ideal," then I too must set myself my own ideal, my own aim. Now, as for a painter or a sculptor or any artist comes the test—what values does the garden-maker try to express? It seems to me that to some extent he has the choice. He may choose the easy way and design a garden as a demonstration of his technical skill and brilliance,…or he may try to make his garden as a symbol…which nature will come to clothe with life.

Sometimes my garden seems like a mirage always receding but if ever this intermittent vision becomes a reality, wherever it is, whatever its size and shape it will be satisfying for like all gardens it will be a world for itself and for me.

Russell Page
The Education of a Gardener, 1962

Gardens of the New World

When Christopher Columbus first caught sight of America, so lush and verdant were its shores that he wrote back to Queen Isabella that he had discovered the Garden of Eden. The first European settlers to arrive in the New World planted gardens in the manner of their homelands. But gradually an American character asserted itself; and, inspired by such avid gardeners as George Washington and Thomas Jefferson, a new American tradition soon flourished.

Thomas Jefferson's Garden Book

Thomas Jefferson had an abiding interest in horticulture and the gardens of his beloved Monticello. He began his "Garden Book," when he was in his early twenties, with notations like "Purple hyacinth begins to bloom; Narcissus and puckoon open"; he continued writing in his garden journal until he was in his eighties. He also corresponded at length with friends about gardening matters, exchanging seeds with George Washington, among others. The acquisition of the Louisiana territories by Jefferson in 1803 had an enormous impact on American gardening as it doubled the size of the country and introduced many new plant types.

On the 27th of February I saw blackbirds and robin-redbreasts, and on the 7th of this month I heard frogs for the first time this year. Have you noted the first appearance of these things at Monticello? I hope you have, and will continue to note every appearance, animal, and vegetable, which indicates the approach of spring, and will communicate them to me. By these means we shall be able to compare the climates of Philadelphia and Monticello. Tell me when you shall have peas, etc., up; when everything comes to table; when you shall have the first chickens hatched; when every kind of tree blossoms, or puts forth leaves; when each kind of flower blooms....

Letter from Thomas Jefferson to his daughter Maria, 9 March 1791

I return to farming with an ardor which I scarcely knew in my youth, and which has got the better entirely of my love of study. Instead of writing ten or twelve letters a day, which I have been in the habit of doing as a thing in course, I put off answering my letters now, farmer-like, till a rainy day…

Letter from Thomas Jefferson
to George Washington, 25 April 1794

I am not yet satisfied that my acquisition of overseers from the head of Elk has been a happy one, or that much will be done this year towards rescuing my plantations from their wretched condition. Time, patience & perseverence must be the remedy; and the maxim of your letter, "slow and sure," is not less a good one in agriculture than in politics.…

Letter from Thomas Jefferson
to George Washington, 14 May 1794

I believe I should be tempted to leave my clover for awhile, to go and hail the dawn of liberty & republicanism in that island. I shall be rendered very happy by the visit you promise me.… If you visit me as a farmer, it must be as a condisciple: for I am but a learner; an eager one indeed, but yet desperate, being too old now to learn a new art. However, I am as much delighted and occupied with it, as if I was the greatest adept. I shall talk with you about it from morning till night, and put you on very short allowance as to political aliment. Now and then a pious ejaculation for the French and Dutch republicans, returning with due des-patch to clover, potatoes, wheat, etc.…

Letter from Thomas Jefferson
to William B. Giles, 27 April 1795

There is no [place] you would be received with more pleasure than at Monticello. Should I be there you will have an opportunity of indulging on a new field some of the taste which has made the Woodlands [Hamilton's estate] the only rival which I have known in America to what may be seen in England.

Thither without a doubt we are to go for models in this art. Their sunless climate has permitted them to adopt what is certainly a beauty of the very first order in landscape. Their canvas is of open ground, variegated with clumps of trees distributed with taste. They need no more of wood than will serve to embrace a lawn or glade. But under the beaming, constant and almost vertical sun of Virginia, shade is our Elysium. In the absence of this no beauty of the eye can be enjoyed. This organ must yield its gratification to that of other senses; without the hope of any equivalent to the beauty relinquished. The only substitute I have been able to imagine is this. Let your ground be covered with trees of the loftiest stature. Trim up their bodies as high as the constitution & form of the tree will bear, but so as that their tops shall unite & yield dense shade. A wood, so open below, will have nearly the appearance of open grounds.…

Letter from Thomas Jefferson
to William Hamilton, July 1806

I have often thought that if heaven had given me choice of my position and calling, it should have been on a rich spot of earth, well watered, and near a good market for the productions of the garden. No occupation is so delightful to me as the culture of the earth, and no culture comparable to that of the garden. Such a variety of subjects, some one always coming to perfection, the failure of one thing repaired by the success of another, and instead of one harvest a continued one through the year. Under a total want of demand except for our family table, I am still devoted to the garden. But though an old man, I am but a young gardener....

Thomas Jefferson to Charles W. Peale, painter and founder of the country's first natural history museum, 20 August 1811

The First Public Parks

By the middle of the 19th century, urban centers were sufficiently overcrowded that a remedy was sought. This became known as the "park movement" and it was spearheaded by a landscape designer from New York's Hudson River Valley, Andrew Jackson Downing. Downing adapted the ideas of Englishman John Claudius Loudon to American tastes. Downing was a fierce believer in "the park" as a democratic retreat for all Americans. He dedicated his important book, A Treatise on the Theory and Practice of Landscape Gardening Adapted to North America *to "John Quincy Adams, ex-President of the United States; the lover of rural pursuits, as well as the distinguished patriot, statesman, and sage."*

We fancy, not without reason, in New-York, that we have a great city, and that the introduction of Croton water, is so marvelous a luxury in the way of health, that nothing more need be done for the comfort of half a million of people. In crossing the Atlantic, a young New-Yorker, who was rabidly patriotic and who boasted daily of the superiority of our beloved commercial metropolis over every city on the globe, was our most amusing companion. I chanced to meet him one afternoon a few days after we landed, in one of the great Parks in London, in the midst of all the sylvan beauty and human enjoyment I have attempted to describe to you. He threw up his arms as he recognized me, and exclaimed—"good heavens! what a scene, and I took some Londoners to the steps of the City Hall last summer, to show them *the Park* of New-York!" I consoled him with the advice to be less conceited thereafter in his cockney-ism, and to show foreigners the Hudson and Niagara, instead of the City Hall and Bowling Green. But the question may well be asked, is New-York really not rich enough, or is there absolutely not land enough in America, to give our citizens public parks of more than ten acres?

Andrew Jackson Downing letter in *Horticulturist,* June 1851

Frederick Law Olmsted

In his twenties the young American farmer Frederick Law Olmsted traveled to England and was greatly impressed by Liverpool's Birkenhead Park.

Walking a short distance up an avenue, we passed through another light iron gate into a thick, luxuriant and diversified garden [Birkenhead Park]. Five minutes of admiration, and a few more spent in studying the manner in which art had been employed to obtain from nature so much beauty, and I was ready to admit that in democratic America there was nothing to be thought of as comparable with this People's Garden. Indeed, gardening had here reached a perfection that I had never before dreamed of. I cannot undertake to describe the effect of so much taste and skill as had evidently been employed; I will only tell you, that we passed by winding paths over acres and acres, with a constant varying surface, where on all sides were growing every variety of shrubs and flowers, with more than natural grace, all set in borders of greenest, closest turf, and all kept with most consummate neatness. At a distance of a quarter of a mile from the gate, we came to an open field of clean, bright green-sward, closely mown, on which a large tent was pitched, and a party of boys in one part, and a party of gentlemen in another, were playing cricket. Beyond this was a large meadow with rich groups of trees, under which a flock of sheep were reposing, and girls and women with children, were playing. While watching the cricketers, we were threatened with a shower, and hastened back to look for shelter, which we found in a pagoda, on an island approached by a Chinese bridge. It was soon filled, as were the other ornamental buildings, by a crowd of those who, like ourselves, had been overtaken in the grounds by the rain; and I was glad to observe that the privileges of the garden were enjoyed about equally by all classes. There were some who were attended by servants, and sent at once for their carriages, but a large proportion were of the common ranks, and a few women with children, or suffering from ill health, were evidently the wives of very humble labourers. There were a number of strangers, and some we observed with notebooks and portfolios, that seemed to have come from a distance to study from the garden. The summer-houses, lodges, bridges, etc., were all well constructed, and of undecaying materials. One of the bridges which we crossed was of our countryman Remington's patent, an extremely light and graceful erection.

Frederick Law Olmsted
Walks and Talks of an American Farmer in England, 1852

New York's Central Park

Two disciples of Andrew Jackson Downing, Olmsted and the English-born Calvert Vaux, teamed up and won the competition to design America's first public park, New York's Central Park.

The Park throughout is a single work of art, and as such subject to the primary law of every work of art, namely, that it shall be framed upon a single, noble motive, to which the design of all its parts, in some more or less subtle way, shall be confluent and helpful.

To find such a general motive of design for the Central Park, it will be necessary to go back to the beginning and ask, for what worthy purpose could the city be required to take out and keep excluded from the field of ordinary urban improvements, a body of land in what was looked forward to as its very centre, so large as that assigned for the Park? For what such object of great prospective importance would a smaller body of land not have been adequate?

It is one great purpose of the Park to supply to the hundreds of thousands of tired workers, who have no opportunity to spend their summers in the country, a specimen of God's handiwork that shall be to them, inexpensively, what a month or two in the White Mountains or the Adirondacks is, at great cost, to those in easier circumstances. The time will come when New York will be built up, when all the grading and filling will be done, and when the picturesquely-varied, rocky formations of the Island will have been converted into formations for rows of monotonous straight street, and piles of erect buildings. There will be no suggestion left of its present varied surface, with the single exception of the few acres contained in the Park. Then the priceless value of the present picturesque outlines of the ground will be more distinctly perceived, and its adaptability for its purpose more fully recognized. It therefore seems desirable to interfere with its easy, undulating outlines, and picturesque, rocky scenery as little as possible, and, on the other hand, to endeavor rapidly, and by every legitimate means, to increase and judiciously develop these particularly individual and characteristic sources of landscape effects.

Considering that large classes of rural objects and many types of natural scenery are not practicable to be introduced on the site of the Park,— mountain, ocean, desert and prairie scenery for example,—it will be found that the most valuable form that could have been prescribed is that which may be distinguished from all others as pastoral. But the site of the Park having had a very heterogeneous surface, which was largely formed of solid rock, it was not desirable that the attempt should be made to reduce it all to the simplicity of pastoral scenery. What would the central motive of design require of the rest? Clearly that it should be given such a character as, while affording contrast and variety of scene, would as much as possible be confluent to the same end, namely, the constant suggestion to the imagination of an unlimited range of rural conditions.

Frederick Law Olmsted and Calvert Vaux
1857

The Bean-Field

Henry David Thoreau lived for two years on the shores of Walden Pond in a cabin that he built himself. While there, he wrote a meditative discourse on how to live life. The lessons to be learned from his virtual "primer" were often couched in puns, allegories, and fables.

Meanwhile my beans, the length of whose rows, added together, was seven miles already planted, were impatient to be hoed, for the earliest had grown considerably before the latest were in the ground; indeed they were not easily to be put off. What was the meaning of this so steady and self-respecting, this small Herculean labor, I knew not. I came to love my rows, my beans, though so many more than I wanted. They attached me to the earth, and so I got strength like Antaeus. But why should I raise them? Only Heaven knows. This was my curious labor all summer,—to make this portion of the earth's surface, which had yielded only cinquefoil, blackberries, johnswort, and the like, before, sweet wild fruits and pleasant flowers, produce instead this pulse. What shall I learn of beans or beans of me? I cherish them, I hoe them, early and late I have an eye to them; and this is my day's work. It is a fine broad leaf to look on. My auxiliaries are the dews and rains which water this dry soil, and what fertility is in the soil itself, which for the most part is lean and effete. My enemies are worms, cool days, and most of all woodchucks. The last have nibbled for me a quarter of an acre clean. But what right had I to oust johnswort and the rest, and break up their ancient herb garden? Soon, however, the remaining beans will be too tough for them, and go forward to meet new foes.

Henry David Thoreau
Walden, or Life in the Woods
1854

Glossary

Based on Michel Conan and Sylvie Brossard, *Dictionnaire Historique de l'Art des Jardins*, 1992, and *The Oxford Companion to Gardens*, 1986. The following definitions are limited to the context of garden and landscape design.

allée a stately tree-lined avenue intended for pedestrian use; the trees are often clipped—or pleached—to form a sort of wall

arboretum a collection of trees planted and cultivated to illustrate the diversity and growth habits of various species and for use in botanical study

Arcadia a central province in the Peloponnese, Greece; traditionally, a pastoral region regarded as a rural paradise of shepherds; idealized by many writers, including Virgil, and painters, including Nicolas Poussin and Claude Lorrain, who in turn were the sources for the *landscape* and *picturesque* gardening styles of 18th-century England

Arts and Crafts movement late 19th-century reaction against the Industrial Revolution and Victorian artifice; in the garden world it led to renewed interest in the craft of gardening, the use of old-fashioned flowers, and a return to the *cottage garden*

avenue a tree-lined passage or road often leading to a manor house; similar to *allée*, but not pedestrian; used in 19th-century city planning

axis an actual or implied straight line used to situate points of view and around which garden elements were arranged. Axes were used in Roman gardens to link the garden and the home, a characteristic that has been copied by landscape architects ever since

bassin a basin or edged pool; important element of French formal gardens

bedding out a system of moving plants from indoor greenhouses, where they have grown during cold months, to outdoor beds in warmer months; see also *change bedding*

belvedere from the Italian for "beautiful view"; a structure that has been carefully sited to command a striking vista

border plantings, usually made in strips, that separate (or soften) garden elements; for example, a thin border along the edges of a flower bed separating the bed from the garden path, or a wide, bushy border softening the effect of a wall. The border was a requisite feature in the gardens of Gertude Jekyll; see also *herbaceous border*

bosco literally, "woods," but often simply a grove of trees in a pleasure garden; by the end of the Renaissance, the *bosco* came to represent the unknown wilderness that lay beyond the civilization of the formal garden

bosquet a tamer version of the Italian *bosco*; a formal grove, often with a decorative glade in which statues and other ornaments could be displayed; especially associated with the gardens of André Le Nôtre

box an evergreen shrub cultivated for hedges, *borders*, and *topiaries*

broderie literally, "embroidery"; a style of planting in flowing shapes that resembles embroidery. See *parterre de broderie*

cabinet de verdure literally, "a room of greenery"; a small, intimate enclosure or "open-air" room within a garden; the "walls" of the enclosure are formed from clipped greenery

carpet bedding the dense, carpet-like planting of beds using dwarf or creeping foliage plants; see also *mosaïculture* and *bedding out*

change bedding artificial system of continually changing the plants in a flower bed so that the beds are always full of greenery and blooming flowers; appealed particularly to the Victorian love of color and ornamentation but was frowned upon by more naturalistic gardeners

cloister the courtyard of a monastery surrounded by a gallery; derived from the layout of the classical Roman villa

conservatory an enclosed usually glazed structure (greenhouse) or room within a house for

sheltering plants over cold seasons and for growing tropical plants in regulated temperature, humidity, and ventilation; a greenhouse was largely the domain of gardeners, whereas a conservatory could be incorporated into a house and could double as a pleasant sitting room. In French and Italian gardens citrus trees were kept indoors in conservatories, or *orangeries* during cold weather; in Victorian England, the popular system of *bedding out* necessitated the cultivation of plants in conservatories in cold weather, which could then be transferred to outdoor beds in warmer months

cottage garden the simple, unpretentious gardens of small homes in rural England; their seemingly casual plantings, often with old-fashioned flowers, greenery, vegetables, and trees influenced middle-class gardening practices during the 19th and 20th centuries

espalier a technique for planting and training the branches of fruit trees to grow flat along trellises or in formal patterns; highly developed in France

ferme ornée although a French term meaning "ornamental farm," it was used to describe a style of landscaping popular in 18th-century England; a functioning farm that has been made decorative by the addition of wide hedgerow paths lined with floral borders and vines

folly a whimsical garden structure that is more decorative than useful

giardino segreto literally, "a secret garden"; an enclosed private garden that derived from the walled gardens of the Middle Ages; particularly prevalent in Italy during the Renaissance

giochi d'acqua literally, "water games" or

"jokes"; water jets in gardens of the Renaissance witch, when activated by unsuspecting visitors, showered them with water. Considered highly entertaining in the 16th century, although they were present in much earlier gardens as well; the jets often also triggered water-powered automata, or moving statuary

greenhouse see *conservatory*

green space modern urban planning term referring to parks, gardens, woodland, or any other planted space set aside for public use

grotto an artificial garden feature designed to simulate a natural grotto or cave; when dedicated to a nymph, and featuring fountains, it is a *nymphaeum*

ha-ha a sunken fence used to demarcate the boundaries of an estate or a landscape without interfering with the view

herbaceous border an artfully planted border of perennial flowers, often along a wall or tall hedge

hortus Latin for "garden"; root of the word horticulture

hortus conclusus literally, an "enclosed garden,"

but came to have religious connotations in the Middle Ages; in the Song of Solomon the Virgin Mary is compared to "a garden enclosed," in reference to her purity

hortus deliciarum literally, "garden of delights"; antithesis of *hortus conclusus;* one of the many names for a pleasure garden (*paradeisos*) whose prototype is the garden of Eden

jardin anglais or **jardin à l'anglaise** literally, "English garden" or "in the English style"; French term for the more naturalistic style of English landscape gardening developed in the 18th century, often used in contrast to the *jardin régulier* or *jardin à la française*—the style of Le Nôtre

jardin anglo-chinois literally, "anglo-Chinese garden"; French expression used to describe the *picturesque* or *landscape* gardens created in England in the 18th century. The French believed that the English landscape garden drew its inspiration from China and sought to undermine its originality with this expression

jardin régulier or **jardin à la française** literally, "regular garden" or "in the French style"; the formal symmetrical French garden of the 17th century whose most characteristic feature is the *broderie de parterre*

kitchen garden garden for growing fruit, vegetables, and herbs for household use; usually situated next

to the home

knot garden elaborate planting of greenery, usually thyme or box, in the shapes of knots; the center of the loops were often filled with brightly colored flowers

labyrinth see *maze*

landscape style term used to describe the gentle, naturalistic approach to garden design (as opposed to the formal French style) that emphasized the larger, sweeping landscape over the smaller flower garden; popularized in England in the 18th century by William Kent and Capability Brown; characterized by sweeping lawns, wooded clumps, and large expanses of water; see also *picturesque style*

maze originally derived from the legend of the Minotaur who was kept by King Minos of Crete in a labyrinth designed by Daedalus; a complex arrangement of paths formed by hedges (also called "hedge mazes") out of which it is difficult to find one's way

mosaïculture French and Belgian technique of the late 1860s that combined carpet bedding with flower bedding. Still seen in French public parks; see also *carpet bedding*

nymphaeum *grotto*, usually with fountains, dedicated to nymphs, or the female nature spirits in Greek and Roman mythology representing the divine powers of lakes, rivers, springs, fountains, seas, mountains and hills, and forests and groves

orangerie *greenhouse* for oranges; building,

usually glazed, for wintering exotic plants. The arrival of highly prized orange trees from China in the 16th century led to a tradition in England of growing plants in glass enclosures

pagoda Far Eastern temple, usually circular, considered fashionable as a garden building in the 18th century

paradeisos enclosed pleasure gardens of Persia that were usually part park, garden, orchard, and hunting ground, stocked with wild game

parterre literally, "on the ground"; a formal plant bed often containing flowers and low hedges laid out geometrically

parterre de broderie literally, "embroidery on the ground"; since the 16th century, a formal bed in which shapes and patterns, usually formed from box, are arranged to create flowing plant-like designs. Developed in France by the Mollet family

patte d'oie in French, "goose foot"; an arrangement of avenues or *allées* radiating from a single point or path, resembling the shape of a goose's foot; in the 17th century often used in front of chateaux

perennial horticultural term usually applied to hardy plants that die down to the ground each year but survive the winter on food stored in specialized underground stems

peristyle Greek architectural element, a covered colonnade, that was copied by the Romans and used

extensively in gardens

perspective technique used since the Renaissance for creating the illusion of distance in painting, stage sets, and gardens

physic garden medieval garden of medicinal plants, usually associated with schools of medicine

picturesque style term used to describe the overtly Romantic landscape designs in 18th-century England that were inspired by the landscape painting of Claude Lorrain, Gaspard Dughet, and Salvator Rosa

pleasure garden see *paradeisos*

portico colonnade used since classical antiquity as a connecting element between a building and a garden; the porticoes surrounding Roman courtyards were often painted with murals; see also *peristyle*

potager see *kitchen garden*

promenade pleasant stroll; also a place for strolling

quincunx literally, "five

twelfths"; an arrangement of trees by fives forming a series of squares or rectangles with a tree at the center of each

topiary since classical antiquity, the art of pruning and shaping trees and shrubs to promote growth or create fanciful shapes

training the controlling of plants, vines, or young trees so that they will grow in a desired shape or direction; see *espalier*

treillage trelliswork; a traditional gardening technique using latticework frames, or *trellises*, to support climbing plants

trellis a fence-like construction against which vines are trained to grow

viridarium an enclosure with fruit-bearing trees, cultivated in the Middle Ages for ornamental purposes; an orchard

woodland underplanting the planting in woodland of native or naturalized species that grow in shade

The Great Gardens of Europe

These outstanding historic gardens are open to the public. The list does not include major public parks.

ITALY

The Italian Lakes and Northwest
Isola Bella, Lake Maggiore
Villa San Remigio, Lake Maggiore
Villa Cicogna, Bisuschio, N of Varese
Villa Carlotta, Lake Como
Villa Balbianello, Lake Como
La Mortola (Giardini Hanbury), W of Ventimiglia
Palazzo Reale, Turin

The Veneto
Villa Barbarigo, Valsanzibio, S of Padua
Botanic Garden of the University of Padua
Villa Rizzardi, NW of Verona, near Negrar
Giardino Giusti, Verona

Tuscany, The Marche, and Emilia Romagna
Boboli Gardens, Florence
Villa La Pietra, N of Florence
Villa Garzoni, Collodi, NE of Lucca
Villa di Castello, Castello, NW of Florence
Villa Pratolino, Pratolino, N of Florence
Villa Reale (Pecci Blunt), Marlia, NE of Lucca
I Tatti, Settignano, NE of Florence
Villa Torrigiani (Santini), Camigliano, NE of Lucca
Castello di Uzzano, Greve in Chianti, S of Florence

Rome and Environs
Palazzo Farnese, Caprarola, SE of Viterbo
Villa Aldobrandini, Frascati, SE of Rome
Villa Lante, Bagnaia, E of Viterbo
Giardino Ninfa, NE of Latina, E of Rome
Villa Orsini (Sacro Bosco), Bomarzo, NE of Viterbo
Villa Giulia (Villa di Papa Giulio), Rome
Villa Madama, Rome
Villa Medici, Rome
Vatican Gardens, Vatican City
Villa d'Este, Tivoli

Campania
Palazzo Reale, Caserta, near Naples
Casa Vettii, Pompeii
Palazzo Rufolo, Ravello, S of Naples

FRANCE

Ile de France and Paris
Chateau de Chantilly, Chantilly, N of Paris
La Maison de Châteaubriand, Châtenay-Malabry, S of Paris
Chateau de Courances, Courances, W of Fontainebleau
Palais de Fontainebleau, Fontainebleau, S of Paris
Chateau de la Malmaison, Reuil-Malmaison, W of Paris
Chateau de Bagatelle, Bois de Boulogne, Paris
Parc Monceau, Paris
Jardin des Plantes, Paris
Chateau de Rambouillet, Rambouillet, SW of Paris
Le Désert de Retz, SW of Chamboury
Parc Jean-Jacques-Rousseau,
Ermenonville, NE of Paris
Chateau de Vaux-le-Vicomte, Maincy, E of Melun
Parc Balbi, Versailles
Trianon (Grand and Petit), Versailles, W of Paris
Chateau de Versailles, Versailles, W of Paris

Brittany, Normandy, and the Loire
Musée Claude Monet, Giverny, E of Vernon
Le Bois des Moutiers, Varengeville-sur-Mer, near Dieppe
Chateau de Brécy, Brécy-Saint-Gabriel, E of Bayeux
Kerdalo, Trédarzec, E of Tréguier
Le Vastérival, W of Varengeville-sur-Mer
Chateau de Villandry, Villandry, W of Tours

Aquitaine, Languedoc, and Central France
Chateau de Hautefort, Hautefort, E of Périgueux

Cote d'Azur, Provence, and the Alps
La Chèvre d'Or, Biot, NW of Antibes
Chateau la Gaude, Les Pinichats, N of Aix-en-Provence
Villa Noailles, W of Grasse
Jardins de la Fondation Ephrussi de Rothschild (Villa Ile de France), St.-Jean-Cap-Ferrat, E of Nice

SPAIN

Pazo de Oca, San Esteban de Oca, SE of Santiago de Compostela
Jardin del Palacio de
Aranjuez, Jardin de la Isla, and Jardin del Principe, S of Madrid
Jardin del Monasterio de El Escorial, NW of Madrid
Jardines de la Granja, La Granja de San Ildefonso, SE of Segovia
El Capricho de la Alameda de Osuna, Madrid
Parque del Buen Retiro, Madrid
Palacio del Prado, N of Madrid
Patio de los Naranjos, Cordoba
Palacio de Viana, Cordoba
Alhambra, Granada
Generalife, Granada
Carmen de los Martires, Granada
Medina Azahara, W of Cordoba
Jardin del Retiro, Alhaurin de la Torre, SW of Malaga
Palacio de las Dueñas, Seville
Jardines de las Reales Alcazares, Seville

PORTUGAL

Quinta da Aveleda, near Paredes, E of Oporto
Quinta da Bacalhôa, W of Setubal
Palacio de Fronteira, Lisbon
Palacio Nacional de Queluz, Queluz, W of Lisbon

GREAT BRITAIN

Southwest England
Blenheim Palace, Woodstock, NW of Oxford
Great Dixter, N of Hastings
Royal Botanic Gardens, Kew, SW of central

London
Chelsea Physic Garden, London
University Botanic Garden, Oxford
Rousham House, Steeple Aston, N of Oxford
Sissinghurst Castle, Sissinghurst, NE of Cranbrook
Stourhead, Stourton, NW of Mere

East Anglia, the Midlands, and Wales
Chatsworth, Bakewell, W of Chesterfield
Hidcote Manor, Hidcote Bartrim, NE of Chipping Campden
Powis Castle, S of Welshpool
Stowe Landscape Gardens, N of Buckingham

Northern England
Levens Hall, SW of Kendal

Scotland
Drummond Castle, between Crieff and Muthill
Inverewe, NE of Gairloch
Little Sparta, SW of Edinburgh

Northern Ireland
Mount Stewart, SE of Newtownards

IRELAND

National Botanic Gardens at Glasnevin, Dublin
Powerscourt, near Enniskerry, S of Dublin
Usher Gardens, Mount Ashford, S of Dublin

BELGIUM

Chateau de Beloeil, SE of Leuze
Kalmthout Arboretum, Kalmthout, N of Antwerp
Kasteel van Leeuwergem, NE of Zottegem

NETHERLANDS

Het Loo, NW of Apeldoorn
Botanic Garden of Leiden University
Kasteel Middachten, De Steeg, E of Arnhem
Walenburg, Langbroek, S of Amersfoort

DENMARK

Fredensborg Slotspark, Fredensborg, N of Copenhagen
Frederiksborg Slotshave, Hillerød, N of Copenhagen
Liselund, E of Borre, NE coast of the Isle of Møn

SWEDEN

Drottningholm, W of Stockholm
Hammarby, SE of Uppsala
Botanic Garden of Uppsala University
The Linnaeus Garden (Linnéträdgården), Uppsala

AUSTRIA

Schloss Hellbrunn, Salzburg
Belvedere, Vienna
Schönbrunn, Vienna

GERMANY

Eremitage, Bayreuth
Schlosspark Nymphenburg, Munich
Park Schloss Schleissheim, Munich
Schloss Veitshöchheim, N of Würzburg
Schlossgarten Schwetzingen, S of Mannheim
Schlossgarten Weikersheim, S of Würzburg
Schlosspark Charlottenburg, Berlin
Park Sanssouci and Charlottenhof Park, Potsdam, SW of Berlin
Wörlitz Park, Wörlitz, E of Dessau

B*roderie* design for the Hortus Palatinus in Heidelberg.

Excerpts from the Florence Charter

The International Committee on Historic Gardens and Sites met in Florence in 1981 to draw up a charter on the preservation of historic gardens. The key articles set forth definitions and objectives dealing primarily with maintenance, conservation, restoration, reconstruction, use, and legal and administrative protection.

Article 1. An historic monument is an architectural and horticultural composition of interest to the public from the historical and artistic point of view.

Article 2. Its constituents are primarily vegetal and therefore living, which means that they are perishable and renewable. Thus its appearance reflects the perpetual balance between the cycle of the seasons, the growth and decay of nature, and the desire of the artist and craftsman to keep it permanently unchanged.

Article 4. The architectural composition of the historic garden includes:
—Its plan and its topography.
—Its vegetation, including its species, proportions, color schemes, spacing, and respective heights.
—Its structural and decorative features.
—Its water, running or still, reflecting the sky.

Article 5. As the expression of the direct affinity between civilization and nature, and as a place of enjoyment suited to meditation or repose, the garden thus acquires the cosmic significance of an idealized image of the world, a "paradise" in the etymological sense of the term, and yet a testimony to a culture, a style, an age, and often to the originality of a creative artist.

Article 6. The term, "historic garden," is equally applicable to small gardens and to large parks, whether formal or "landscape."

Article 9. The preservation of historic gardens depends on their identification and listing. They require several kinds of action, namely maintenance, conservation and restoration. In certain cases, reconstruction may be recommended. The *authenticity* of an historic garden depends as much on the design and scale of its various parts as on its decorative features and on the choice of plant or inorganic materials adopted for each of its parts.

Further Reading

Acton, Harold, *Great Houses of Italy: The Tuscan Villas,* Viking Press, New York, 1973

Adams, William Howard, *Nature Perfected: Gardens Through History,* Abbeville Press, New York, 1991

———, *The French Garden, 1500–1800,* George Braziller, New York, 1979

Bazin, Germain, *Paradeisos: The Idea of a Garden,* Little Brown, Boston, 1990

Best, Clare, and Caroline Boisset, eds., *Leaves from the Garden: Two Centuries of Garden Writing,* Norton, New York, 1987

Bisgrove, Richard, *The Gardens of Gertrude Jekyll,* Little Brown, Boston, 1992

Brown, Jane, *The Art and Architecture of English Gardens,* Weidenfeld and Nicolson, London, 1989

———, *Gardens of a Golden Afternoon. The Story of a Partnership: Edwin Lutyens and Gertrude Jekyll,* Van Nostrand Reinhold, New York, 1982

———, *Eminent Gardeners: Some People of Influence and Their Gardens, 1880–1980,* Viking, New York, 1990

———, *Sissinghurst: Portrait of a Garden,* Harry N. Abrams, New York, 1990

Chambers, Douglas, *The Planters of the English Landscape Garden,*
Yale University Press, New Haven, 1993

Chatfield, Judith, *The Classic Italian Garden,* Rizzoli, New York, 1991

———, *A Tour of Italian Gardens,* Rizzoli, New York, 1988

Cowell, F. R., *The Garden as Fine Art from Antiquity to Modern Times,* Houghton Mifflin, Boston, 1978

Hazlehurst, F. Hamilton, *Gardens of Illusion: The Genius of André Le Nostre,* Vanderbilt University Press, Nashville, 1980

Hobhouse, Penelope, *Plants in Garden History,* Pavilion, London, 1992

———, and Patrick Taylor, eds., *The Gardens of Europe,* Random House, New York, 1990

Hunt, John Dixon, *Garden and Grove,* Princeton University Press, Princeton, 1986

———, and Peter Willis, *The Genius of the Place,* MIT Press, Cambridge, 1988

Hussey, Christopher, *English Gardens and Landscapes, 1700–1750,* Country Life Books, London, 1967

Hyams, Edward, *Capability Brown and Humphry Repton,* Scribner's, New York, 1971

Jellicoe, Geoffrey, Susan Jellicoe, Patrick Goode, and
Michael Lancaster, eds., *The Oxford Companion to Gardens,* Oxford University Press, Oxford and New York, 1986

Lazzaro, Claudia, *The Italian Renaissance Garden,* Yale University Press, New Haven and London, 1990

MacDougall, Elisabeth, ed., *Ancient Roman Villa Gardens,* Dumbarton Oaks, Washington, D.C., 1987

———, and Richard Ettinghausen, eds., *The Islamic Garden,* Dumbarton Oaks, Washington, D.C., 1976

Masson, Georgina, *Italian Gardens,* Harry N. Abrams, New York, 1961

Moore, Charles W., William J. Mitchell, and William Turnbull, Jr., *The Poetics of Gardens,* MIT Press, Cambridge, 1988

Mosser, Monique, and Georges Teyssot, eds., *The Architecture of Western Gardens: A Design History from the Renaissance to the Present Day,* MIT Press, Cambridge, 1991

Ottewill, David, *The Edwardian Garden,* Yale University Press, New Haven and London, 1989

Page, Russell, *The Education of a Gardener,* Random House, New York, 1983

Pevsner, Nikolaus, ed., *The Picturesque Garden and Its Influence Outside the British Isles,* Dumbarton Oaks,
Washington, D.C., 1974

Scott-James, Anne, *Sissinghurst: The Making of a Garden,* Michael Joseph, London, 1974

Scully, Vincent, *Architecture: the Natural and the Manmade,* St. Martin's Press, New York, 1991

Shepherd, J. C., and G. A. Jellicoe, *Italian Gardens of the Renaissance,* Princeton University Press, Princeton, 1986 (1st pub. 1925)

Thacker, Christopher, *The History of Gardens,* University of California Press, Berkeley and Los Angeles, 1979

Triggs, Harry Inigo, *Formal Gardens in England and Scotland* (1st publ. London, 1902), Antique Collectors' Club, 1988

Turner, Roger, *Capability Brown,* Rizzoli, New York, 1985

Van Zuylen, Gabrielle, *The Gardens of Russell Page,* Stewart, Tabori & Chang, New York, 1991

Watkin, David, *The English Vision: The Picturesque in Architecture, Landscape, and Design,* Harper and Row, New York, 1982

Wharton, Edith, *Italian Villas and Their Gardens,* The Century Company, New York, 1904

Woodbridge, Kenneth, *Princely Gardens: The Origins and Development of the French Formal Style,* Rizzoli, New York, 1986

List of Illustrations

Index

Acknowledgments

The author extends her heartfelt thanks to Frédéric Morvan for his assistance and friendship. The publisher wishes to thank Marie-Thérèse Gousset (Manuscript Division) and Sylvie Aubenas (Print Division) of the Bibliothèque Nationale de France, as well as Pierre Brulé.

Photograph Credits

Copyright © by ADAGP Paris 1994 112–3. All rights reserved 1–7, 54b, 60a, 77, 82a, 86, 88, 90, 92b, 103b, 119b, 121r, 127, spine. Archiv für Kunst und Geschichte, Berlin 63, 106l. Artothek/Peissenberg 40–1. Bibliothèque Nationale, Paris 28, 31, 33b, 34l, 35a, 37b, 39, 43b, 46, 47a, 55, 60–1b, 61a, 66l–r, 67b, 68a, 69, 74b, 75b, 76a–b 78a–b, 79b, 91a, 97a, 107, 111b, 114, 134, 135, 138, 140, 141, 144, 146, 148, 154, 161, 162, 163, 165. Bibliothèque Royale Albert 1er, Brussels 42l. Bodleian Library, Oxford 35b, 36, 38b, 85a. British Library, London 25r. British Museum, London 15a, 57a, 130. Bulloz, Paris 17b, 20–1a, 66b, 93. Christie's Images, London 84–5b, 103a. Martin Classen, Cologne 58–9a. Dagli-Orti, Paris 21b, 23, 26b, 32–3a, 34r, 37a, 38a, 42r, 44, 50, 51a, 52, 53b, 57b–l, 64, 80, 81, 108. Edimédia, Paris 26a, 96, 115. Ecole Nationale Supérieure des Beaux-Arts, Paris 18. E.T. Archives, London 87a, 94. Explorer, Vanves 43a, 106r. Explorer/Lipnitzki 48a. Explorer/Mary Evans 102a. Explorer/Peter Willi 129. Gallimard/Jacques Sassier 8. Giraudon, Vanves 29, 36c, 67a, 74–5a, 83, 91b. Ikona/F. Danesin 56. Ikona/M. Fugenzi 51b. Ikona/De Luca 53a. Ikona/C. Mattoni 57b–r. Erica Lennard 123a, 128. Jane Lidz front cover. Mise au Point/Yann Monel, Ivry 120. Museum van Het Loo/E. Boeijinja 79a. Musées Royaux des Beaux-Arts de Belgique 48–9b. Metropolitan Museum of Art, New York 15b. Musées de la Ville de Paris, Copyright © by SPADEM 1994 110, 111a. National Portrait Gallery, London 89b. National Trust Photo Library, London 87b, 121l. Parcs et Jardins de la Ville de Paris 124–5. Rapho/Jacques Faujour 126. Réunion des Musées Nationaux, Paris 9, 11, 12, 16, 19, 25r, 32b, 62, 65a–b, 68b, 70, 71, 72–3, 104–5, 116, 132. Roger-Viollet, Paris 13, 14, 92a, 112, 113. Royal Institute of British Architects, London 109, 118. Royal Horticultural Society, London 54a, 97b, 98–9, 100–1, 119a, 151, 152. Scala, Florence 10, 17a, 20b, 22, 27, 30, 45, 47b, 59b, 65c, 131, back cover. Marina Schinz 117, 122. Science Museum, London 102b. Tate Gallery, London 89a. Top/Desjardins 123b. Top/Jarry-Tripelon 95, 125b. Victoria and Albert Museum, London 24–5, 82b. Claire de Virieu, Paris 124b.

Text Credits

Grateful acknowledgment is made for use of material from the following works: Chrétien de Troyes, *The Complete Romances of Chrétien de Troyes*, trans. David Staines, Indiana University Press, 1990. Columella, Lucius Junius Moderatus, *On Agriculture and Trees*, vol. III, book X, trans. E.S. Forster and Edward H. Heffner, Cambridge, Mass.: Harvard University Press, 1955. Reprinted by permission of the publishers and the Loeb Classical Library. Goethe, Johann Wolfgang von, *Elective Affinities*, trans. Elizabeth Mayer and Louise Bogan, with an Introduction by Victoria Lange. Copyright © 1963 by Regnery Publishing, Inc. All rights reserved. Reprinted by special permission of Regnery Publishing, Inc., Washington, D.C. Guillaume de Lorris and Jean de Meun, *The Romance of the Rose*, trans. Charles Dahlberg, Princeton University Press, 1971. Homer, *The Odyssey of Homer* (p. 114), trans. Richard Lattimore. Copyright © 1965, 1967 by Richard Lattimore. Copyright renewed. Reprinted by permission of HarperCollins Publishers Inc. Hunt, John Dixon and Peter Willis, eds., *The Genius of the Place*, The MIT Press, 1988. Jefferson, Thomas, *Thomas Jefferson's Garden Book*, The American Philosophical Society, 1985. Used with permission of the publisher. Masson, Georgina, *Italian Gardens*, Harry N. Abrams, Inc., New York. Used with permission of the publisher. Montaigne, Michel de, *The Complete Works of Montaigne: Essays, Travel Journal, Letters*, trans. Donald M. Frame, with permission of the publishers, Stanford University Press. Copyright © 1943 by Donald M. Frame, copyright © 1948, 1957 by the Board of Trustees of the Leland Stanford Junior University. Olmsted, Frederick Law, Jr., and Theodora Kimball, eds., *Frederick Law Olmsted*, Benjamin Blom, Inc./Ayer Co. Publishers, Inc., 1970. Page, Russell, *The Education of a Gardener*. Copyright © 1962. Reprinted by permission of Random House, Inc. Pliny, *The Letters of the Younger Pliny*, trans. Betty Radice (Penguin Classics 1963, revised edition, 1969). Copyright © 1963, 1969 by Betty Radice. Rousseau, Jean-Jacques, *La Nouvelle Héloïse* (Julie, or the New Eloise, Letters of Two Lovers, Inhabitants of a Small Town at the Foot of the Alps), trans. and abridg. Judith H. McDowell, University Park, The Pennsylvania State University Press, 1968, pp. 306, 311, 312. Copyright © 1968 by The Pennsylvania State University. Reproduced by permission of the publisher. Sackville-West, Vita, in *Observer*, August 25, 1957. Copyright © Nigel Nicolson, executor to Vita Sackville-West. Scully, Vincent, *Architecture: The Natural and the Manmade*. Copyright © 1991 by Vincent Scully. Reprinted with permission of St. Martin's Press. Stoppard, Tom, *Arcadia*, Faber and Faber Ltd., 1993. Copyright © Tom Stoppard, 1993. Used with permission of the publisher. Thoreau, Henry David, *Walden*, 1st edition, reproduced in Norton Anthology of Literature, 1979. Virgil, *Georgics*, trans. Smith Palmer Bovie, The University of Chicago Press. Copyright © 1956 by The University of Chicago. Woodbridge, Kenneth, *Princely Gardens*, Thames & Hudson Ltd., copyright © 1986 Kenneth Woodbridge.

Gabrielle van Zuylen was born in France
and educated in the United States. She co-authored
with Anita Pereire *Jardins Privés de France* (Arthaud,
1984, preface by Russell Page), which was awarded
a prize by the Académie Française. In 1991 the Garden
Writers Association of America named her second book,
The Gardens of Russell Page (Stewart, Tabori & Chang, 1992),
"the best book on gardens." She is a member
of the International Dendrological Society,
Les Amateurs des Jardins, and is a Chevalier of
the Ordre National du Mérite Agricole.
She is also a gardener.

To Françoise and my four daughters

Translated from the French by I. Mark Paris

For Harry N. Abrams, Inc.
Editor: Sarah Burns
Typographic Designer: Elissa Ichiyasu
Design Supervisor: Miko McGinty
Assistant Designer: Tina Thompson
Text Permissions: Neil Ryder Hoos

Library of Congress Catalog Card Number: 95-75671

ISBN 0-8109-2851-5

Copyright © 1994 Gallimard

English translation copyright © 1995 Harry N. Abrams, Inc., New York,
and Thames and Hudson Ltd., London

Published in 1995 by Harry N. Abrams, Inc., New York
A Times Mirror Company

Printed and bound in Italy by Editoriale Libraria, Trieste